508.9.   dodd.m.

DATE DUE

THE NEW
EXPLORERS

Women
in
Antarctica

Books by Barbara Land

THE NEW EXPLORERS

EVOLUTION OF A SCIENTIST

Barbara Land

THE NEW EXPLORERS

Women
in
Antarctica

Illustrated with photographs

DODD, MEAD & COMPANY
New York

Illustrations courtesy of: Rosemary Askin, 90, 91, 97, 99; Australia's Wildlife Heritage series published by The Rigby Group, 93, 94–95; Katharine Cashman, 203, 209, 213; Charlene Denys, 72; Yuan DeVries, 109; Gisela Dreschhoff, 170; Imre Friedmann, 191, 194; Lois Jones, 13, 45, 46 *bottom*, 51, 52; Ursula Marvin, 177; Rita Mathews, 119 *left;* Christine Muller-Schwarze, 26; Dietland Muller-Schwarze, 25, 35, 70; NASA, 180, 185, 187; New Zealand Antarctic Society, 10; John Oliver, 141 *right,* 144; Irene Peden, 76; Julie Ann Samson, 218; United States Navy, 19, 20, 39, 40–41, 46 *top,* 87 *top,* 112, 115 *right,* 119 *right,* 126, 129, 132 *bottom,* 136, 141 *left,* 156, 197; United States Navy. Photo by Babin, 115 *left,* 216 *right;* United States Navy. Photo by Wade A. Davis, 75, 82, 87 *bottom;* United States Navy. Photo by Jim Haus, 165; United States Navy. Photo by Hilton, 127, 132 *top,* 162, 167; United States Navy. Photo by Michael Jacobs, 220 *top;* United States Navy. Photo by Kyne, 148, 149, 159; United States Navy. Photo by Thomas McCabe, 32; United States Navy. Photo by Martell, 118; United States Navy. Photo by Nortell, 216 *left;* United States Navy. Photo by R. Payne, 29, 107; United States Navy. Photo by Eugene Smith, 56, 64, 66; United States Navy. Photo by K. K. Thornsley, 63, 104, 139, 153; United States Navy. Photo by J. A. Warning, 206; United States Navy. Photo by Weinger, 215; University of Minnesota, 124, 220 *bottom;* Edward Zeller, 174.

1 2 3 4 5 6 7 8 9 10

Library of Congress Cataloging in Publication Data

Land, Barbara.
    The new explorers, women in Antarctica.

    Includes index.
    1. Antarctic regions—Discovery and exploration.
2. Explorers, Women. 3. Women scientists. I. Title.
G860.L35   508.98'9   80–39529
ISBN 0–396–07924–5

For Mike

and our young explorers

Author's Note

The women introduced in this book made the whole thing possible by telling me their stories and patiently explaining their work. But first I had to find them.

My search began in Christchurch, New Zealand, where early clues came from James M. Caffin of the New Zealand Antarctic Society; Chief Journalist William Neal, Jr., of the U.S. Navy Operation Deep Freeze; Margaret Lanyon, National Science Foundation representative in New Zealand; and Walter Seelig, International Coordinator for the NSF Division of Polar Programs. Other valuable information was provided by Colin Monteath of the DSIR and Philip Kyle, then at Victoria University of Wellington.

In Washington, D.C., my questions were answered by Guy Guthridge, Jack Renirie, and Ralph Kazarian of the National Science Foundation and—again—by Walter Seelig. More help was given by Ruth Siple and Richard Darley, then at the National Geographic Society; Gerald Pagano at the National Archives; and the late William R. MacDonald, Chief of the Topographic Division of the U.S. Geological Survey.

Other clues were offered by Dr. Jay T. Shurley and Dr. Harold G. Muchmore of the University of Oklahoma Medical Center and by Professors Campbell Craddock, University of Wisconsin-Madison; Theodore Foster, University of California-Santa Cruz; Thomas S. Laudon, University of Wisconsin-Oshkosh; and Joseph Warburton, University of Nevada Desert Research Institute, Reno.

Special thanks go to Elaine K. Houser of Holmes and Narver, Inc., who helped me find people during two USARP orientation meetings in Washington, and to Eugene R. Smith, the U.S. Navy photographer who took pictures in Antarctica especially for this book.

Barbara Land

CONTENTS

One

FROZEN LABORATORY

"There are some things women don't do," Harry Darlington told his bride. "They don't become Pope or President—or go down to the Antarctic."

A reasonable statement—in 1947—but Jennie Darlington was upset. Just a few weeks after their wedding, her husband was going away to the bottom of the world for a full year. Why couldn't she go along? There wasn't much comfort in the argument that all the heroic polar explorers of the past had left their wives at home.

Soon after that conversation, Jennie's wish came true and the Darlingtons became part of Antarctic history. Jennie wrote about her adventures in *My Antarctic Honeymoon,* a breezy account of her year on the frozen continent. It wasn't all fun. A few narrow escapes and a winter of ill-feeling convinced her that her husband had been right in the first place.

"Taking everything into consideration," she wrote, "I do not think women belong in Antarctica."

For the next twenty years the United States Navy agreed with Jennie Darlington and refused to transport women to U.S.

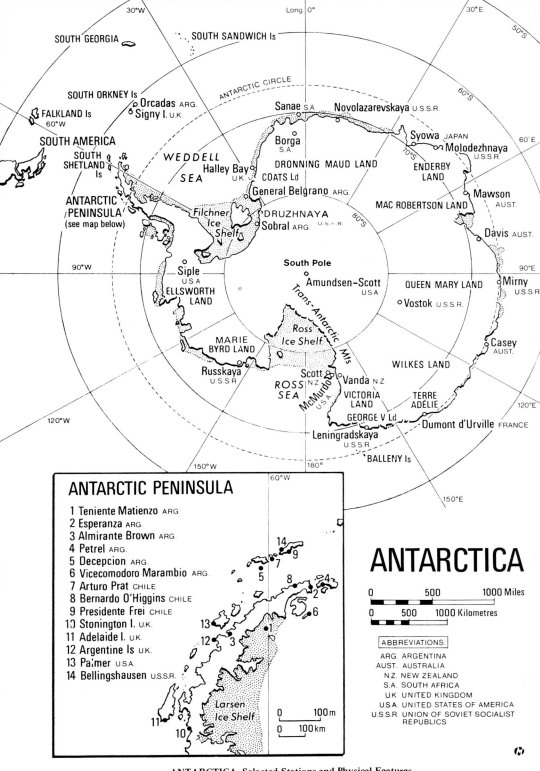

ANTARCTICA Selected Stations and Physical Features

research stations in Antarctica. A few determined scientists disagreed with Jennie and the Navy. Their patience and determination finally paid off. Today dozens of women work in Antarctica as research scientists, medical doctors, technicians, and administrators.

Jeanette Thomas has spent so much time on the ice with Weddell seals that she sometimes understands what they are saying to each other.

Nan Scott travels to the South Pole twice a year to collect blood samples from the arms of people who work at this most isolated research station on earth. She and her colleagues have made surprising discoveries about the effects of isolation on human immunities to disease.

Katharine Cashman knows how it feels to be inside the crater of a volcano when it erupts.

Roseli Ocampo traveled south to collect microscopic plants hidden inside Antarctic rocks. She watched them grow in laboratory cultures and disproved forever the assumption that nothing could live in the Antarctic desert. Her work also changed the expectations of space scientists who wonder if life exists on Mars.

All these women are scientists and all are relative newcomers to Antarctica. Traditionally, the southernmost continent was a place for men only. Men discovered it and men explored it. For 150 years after the first explorers went ashore in 1821, it was a womanless world, except for a handful of visitors. Not until the 1970s were women accepted as equal partners in science on a continent reserved for science.

This exclusive dedication to science came about after the International Geophysical Year, 1957, when earth scientists from all over the world worked together to answer basic questions about this planet. They drilled holes in the ocean floor, climbed volcanoes, and set out to explore and map every bit of uncharted land they could find—especially Antarctica.

Because it was remote, unspoiled, and mostly unmapped, Antarctica was a perfect natural laboratory. It became a big, friendly, international community of scientists who pooled their information; shared planes, ships, tractors, and lab space; and tried to learn each other's languages.

During the IGY, international cooperation worked so well that scientists persuaded their governments to sign a treaty—the Antarctic Treaty of 1959. All countries with territorial claims on the continent were asked to forget about them for at least thirty years. When the treaty was signed in 1959, Antarctica became the only place on earth where national boundaries did not exist. It is still the only place on earth set aside exclusively for scientists.

Nothing was said about excluding *women* scientists, but that was the way things were for nearly a decade after the treaty was signed. American women scientists who pioneered had to overcome U.S. Navy regulations that kept them out of American research stations. As soon as a few women demonstrated their competence as polar scientists, others found acceptance.

It may be easier to imagine these women at work after a brief geography lesson and a little history. On a library globe, Antarctica is at the very bottom—not easy to see unless you lift the globe or stoop low enough to look up at it. If the globe is an old one, Antarctica is only a white blob surrounding the bolt that fastens the globe to its axis. The South Pole is somewhere under the bolt. Around the continent, the waters of three oceans meet and mingle.

Maybe it looks small on the map, but Antarctica is huge—about five million square miles—as big as the United States

Women scientists at work in Antarctica

and Mexico combined. Most of it is permanently buried under ice and snow. In some spots the ice is almost three miles thick. Nobody has ever seen the shape of the land under all that ice, but scientists have been able to construct a fairly accurate picture of rugged mountain ranges.

The combination of high mountains and the enormous accumulation of ice has made Antarctica the highest of all continents. It is also the coldest—too cold for trees and animals. Too cold, even, for disease germs. Sea animals that come ashore in summer could not survive in the interior where temperatures never climb above freezing and sometimes drop to minus 80 degrees Centigrade. Raging winds, in every season, make the climate even more hostile.

Very little was known about Antarctica until this century. Nobody had even seen it until about 1820. For hundreds of years before that, explorers had tried to find it.

At first it was only a theory. Ancient Greek geographers—who believed in the perfect symmetry of nature—speculated that there must be a large mass of land at the bottom of the earth to balance known lands at the top. Centuries later, maps showed a southern hemisphere half covered by a large body of land labeled *Terra Australis*—or Southern Land.

This old globe from 1860 text-book hardly hints at a land at the bottom of the world.

Then Antarctica became a legend. In the sixteenth and seventeenth centuries, Portuguese, Spanish, and Dutch ships searched for a southern paradise rich in gold and timber.

Captain James Cook, the British explorer who came closest to the southern continent in 1773, never saw it through the fog and almost erased it from the maps. He wrote: "We are now sure that no Southern Continent exists there, unless so near the pole that the Coast cannot be navigated for Ice and therefore not worth the discovery. . . ."

Captain Cook found no polar gold, but he reported wealth of another kind. The icy southern waters were rich in sea life—especially huge colonies of seals and whales. In those days, before the invention of electric lights, whale oil lamps illuminated the world. Seal furs brought high prices from the fashion capitals of Europe and America. Whaling ships and seal hunters raced southward, following Captain Cook's charts.

They slaughtered the whales and stained the snow-covered islands red with the blood of seals. If any of them saw a large body of land through the fog, they didn't give away the secret source of their rich cargoes.

Who was first to see the Antarctic continent? Historians disagree. Maybe it was Nathaniel Palmer, an American sea captain. Or maybe it was the Russian explorer, Captain Thaddeus von Bellinghausen. Both were sailing in the area during the latter part of 1820 and early in 1821. Both reported sighting the Antarctic peninsula—that curving finger of land that reaches toward the tip of South America.

Old print shows the United States Exploring Expedition—Charles Wilkes, Esq., Commander—landing on the Antarctic continent, January 19, 1840.

Neither Palmer nor Bellinghausen went ashore but both reported the discovery. The first landing was claimed separately
by French, British, and American explorers and was disputed
for years until a forgotten logbook settled the argument.

John Davis of Connecticut, captain of the American sealer
Cecilia, took a landing party ashore on February 7, 1821. His
logbook entry was very specific about the date. He was also
first to make the flat statement: "I think this southern land to
be a continent."

Seventy-five years later, Antarctica was still considered "the
greatest piece of geographical exploration still to be under-
taken." At an International Geographical Congress meeting in
London in 1895, explorers of all countries were challenged to
penetrate the barrier of ice—to reach the South Pole. Men who
took up the challenge became the heroes of Antarctic legend.

The British explorers Robert Falcon Scott and Ernest Shackle-
ton, Australia's Douglas Mawson, Norway's Roald Amundsen,
and America's Admiral Richard E. Byrd all made and wrote
the history of a new continent. Their true accounts—stories
of danger, discovery and heroism—are among the most exciting
adventure books on library shelves. Apsley Cherry-Garrard, a
survivor of Scott's 1910 expedition, called it *The Worst Journey
in the World*—but he later remembered the experience as the
high point of his life.

Women had no part in these early explorations. They were
left at home for more than a hundred years—until the first
woman finally stepped ashore on the Antarctic continent in 1935.

Caroline Mikkelsen, wife of a Norwegian whaling captain,
accompanied her husband on a voyage to the Antarctic. Klarius
Mikkelsen's ship, one of a fleet directed by Lars Christiansen,
was not at all like the fragile sailing vessels that carried earlier

explorers. It was a sturdy factory ship, big enough to carry airplanes to look for whales as well as all the heavy equipment necessary for processing whale oil.

On February 20, 1935, the captain and his wife went ashore in a small boat, landing on the eastern coast of Antarctica, near the present location of Australia's Davis Station. They looked around briefly; then Caroline was taken back to the ship.

Two years later, Christiansen himself went down to see his ships at work. The whaling magnate's wife and daughter and two of their female friends went along. Now, on any detailed map of Antarctica, you can find Four Ladies Bank, just off the Ingrid Christensen Coast—permanent reminders that women were among the early Antarctic tourists.

No other women visited the continent until 1947 when Edith Ronne and Jennie Darlington spent a whole year with their husbands on Stonington Island near the Antarctic Peninsula.

Finn Ronne, a Norwegian-American explorer who had accompanied Admiral Byrd's expeditions in 1933 and 1939, organized his own private expedition soon after the end of World War II. As his aviation chief, he appointed a young U.S. Naval Officer, Harry Darlington.

It was an all-male venture, traveling by ship, but Ronne's wife, Edith, was allowed to accompany the group part of the way to write news reports for North American Newspaper Alliance. Darlington, just married, was invited to bring his 22-year-old bride, Jennie. The two women were expected to leave the ship at Valparaiso, Chile, the last port before Antarctica.

At the last minute, Commander Ronne decided that his wife's newspaper stories were important to the expedition. Edith Ronne was to stay with the ship, so Jennie Darlington was asked to come along, too.

In November, 1947, the Darlingtons set up their first home at one end of a bunkhouse they shared with twenty men. Young Jennie found herself playing mother to the whole brood. She listened to their troubles, tried to mediate their squabbles, and wished they'd stop adding their socks to her laundry. She learned how to drive a dog team, how to melt ice for bath water, how to survive.

It wasn't an easy life, even at the best of times. For Jennie it became downright bleak after her husband and the expedition leader had a series of heated arguments over flight operations. When Harry Darlington was grounded, Jennie sided with her husband and lost the friendship of the only other woman in Antarctica.

"Imagine yourself on a spaceship in another world," she wrote later, "a world that for ten million years had been locked away behind ramparts of ice and where escape is blocked in all directions by a cold, cruel sea."

Jennie Darlington started thinking about "escape" when she and Harry were expecting their first child. In October, 1948, nearly a year after their arrival on Stonington Island, the ship that was to have taken them home was frozen in the ice and refused to budge. The Darlingtons' daughter almost became the first child born in Antarctica.

A last-minute rescue by two U.S. Navy icebreakers made it possible for the Darlingtons to return to Virginia just in time for the baby's birth. The first native Antarctican wouldn't be born for another thirty years. Emilio Marcos Palma was born, January 7, 1978, at Argentina's Esperanza Base, to the wife of the chief officer.

After the Ronne expedition, more than twenty years passed before any other American women lived and worked on the

Icebreakers plow through the Ross Sea to McMurdo Station.

Antarctic continent. After the IGY and the signing of the Antarctic Treaty, more and more scientists—both men and women—became involved in Antarctic research. But women were obliged to do their research at a distance, to depend upon male colleagues and male students to set up equipment and bring back samples. Why, these women asked, were they kept out of the world's largest international research laboratory?

Before their questions were answered, a Russian marine geologist became the first woman scientist to do research in Antarctica.

Professor Marie V. Klenova, a member of the Council for Antarctic Research of the USSR Academy of Sciences, had worked in the northern polar regions for nearly thirty years. In the austral summer of 1956, she went south with a Soviet oceanographic team to map uncharted areas of the Antarctic coast. Her findings became part of the first Antarctic atlas, an impressive four-volume work published in the Soviet Union.

For most of the season, Dr. Klenova made shipboard observations from the Russian icebreakers *Ob* and *Lena.* Between voyages she worked at Mirny, a Russian base on the Queen Mary Coast, an area shared by Australian and Polish research stations.

While U.S. stations in Antarctica were still womanless, a Chicago biologist—Dr. Mary Alice McWhinnie—was gaining a worldwide reputation as an Antarctic scientist. She became an expert on the shrimplike krill, favorite food of whales, seals, and penguins.

Without setting foot on forbidden territory, Dr. McWhinnie cruised the Antarctic oceans aboard a floating laboratory, the United States research ship *Eltanin.* Summer after austral summer, between 1962 and 1972, she worked at sea. When she finally landed to work on the Antarctic continent she became

Aerial view of McMurdo Station

the first woman ever to head an Antarctic research station. As chief scientist at McMurdo, the largest U.S. station in Antarctica, she shared the isolation of a six-month polar night with one other woman, Sister Mary Odile Cahoon, and about a hundred men.

But before all barriers were lifted by the U.S. Navy, some other countries were taking tentative steps toward including women in their Antarctic research programs. In the southern summer of 1968–69, four Argentine women did hydrographic research along the Antarctic Peninsula. All were veteran scientists. Professors Irene Bernasconi, Maria Adela Caria, Elena Martinez Fontes, and Carmen Pujals added their names to the list of pioneers.

Meanwhile, there were rumors in the United States that Navy policy was about to change. Plans for building a women's barracks at McMurdo were announced—then promptly denied by the admiral in charge. Rear Admiral Fred E. Bakutis, then commander of Operation Deep Freeze, the task force for the National Science Foundation's Antarctic Research Program, said the Navy would be asking for trouble if women were allowed to work at McMurdo.

Officials at the National Science Foundation in Washington were convinced that a change was inevitable. A few women scientists were encouraged to submit proposals for Antarctic research.

Finally, during the 1969–70 season, the first women were included in the United States Antarctic Research Program. Lois Jones, a geochemist at Ohio State University, was invited to head a four-woman team of researchers—women only.

Dr. Jones and her companions—Terry Lee Tickhill, Eileen McSaveney, and Kay Lindsay—pitched their tents in a rocky

Antarctic valley and started to work. During the season a fifth woman, reporter Jean Pearson of *The Detroit News,* visited their field camp for a few days, becoming the first woman journalist to visit Antarctica since Edith Ronne's impromptu visit twenty-two years earlier.

Once the continent had opened to a few women, it didn't take long for them to win the respect of their male colleagues. Women, it seemed, could survive the hostile climate. Women would not necessarily "go to pieces" in a crisis, or fight with each other, or complain of boredom. Soon they found themselves accepted as equals. Even, sometimes, as leaders.

This was no surprise to some of the men involved in Antarctic science. Many of them were accustomed to working with female colleagues in university laboratories. Some of them were married to scientists who shared their research. As soon as restrictions were removed, these men wanted to bring their wives to Antarctica as co-workers or field assistants.

A number of husband-and-wife teams eventually worked together on the ice. The first of these, Dietland and Christine Muller-Schwarze from Utah State University, spent three Antarctic summers together studying the behavior of penguins. Their first summer began in October, 1969, a few weeks before the arrival of Lois Jones and her all-woman team.

There was no race to see who would be first. All the women were eager to begin their work on the continent, but circumstances—such as the nesting habits of penguins—settled the priority. Christine Muller-Schwarze got there first.

Two

AT HOME WITH 300,000 PENGUINS

A small welcoming committee—six Adélie penguins—greeted Christine and Dietland Muller-Schwarze when they stepped down from the helicopter at Cape Crozier. The curious birds came running toward the strangers, waving their flippers and calling a raucous *ark, ark.* A few feet away, they stopped and tilted their heads to regard the newcomers, first with one eye, then with the other.

Christine met the penguins with equal curiosity. For the next ten weeks these birds would be her close neighbors and daily companions. At the end of three Antarctic summers she would know them better than she knew her human neighbors in Utah.

In mid-October of 1969, Christine Muller-Schwarze, a German-born Ph.D. psychologist, was the only woman at work with the U.S. research program on the Antarctic continent.

The barriers were down at last. Other women were about to arrive—the four-woman geology team from Ohio, a New Zealand biologist, and a journalist from Detroit—but Christine had landed first. She and Dietland had made the eight-hour flight from Christchurch, New Zealand, to McMurdo with the season's first planeload of Antarctic scientists.

"We weren't trying to set any records," she said later. "We just wanted to be at Cape Crozier when the first penguins arrived to choose their nesting sites."

Although the six Adélies were there ahead of them, the scientists arrived in plenty of time to watch the slopes of Cape Crozier fill up, during the next few days, with thousands and thousands of noisy, busy, endlessly fascinating penguins.

"My husband had begun the work several years earlier, before women were permitted to work on the continent," Christine explained. "He is an ethologist—a zoologist who specializes in animal behavior. In Utah we worked as a team, investigating scent communication among deer and antelope. When Dietland received a grant from the National Science Foundation to continue his penguin studies in Antarctica, it seemed only natural that I should accompany him."

Her husband agreed. "I wanted her to come along for many reasons," he said. "Oh, of course there were people who said, 'If you take your wife, you won't get much work done'—but we found the opposite was true. We work very efficiently together. We know each other very well—know what to expect— are able to work without stopping to explain every step. That summer we had a very short time to do a lot of work. But we didn't have to waste time getting acquainted with other people's work habits."

Instead, they got acquainted with the penguins. By the hundreds, the energetic little birds came in from the sea, leaping vertically out of the water and landing feet first on the ice cliff. In seemingly joyful processions, they marched across the ice, sometimes leaning forward to coast on their bellies, like children on sleds. Gradually they filled the rocky slopes, until the hills became a crowded penguin city.

Christine Muller-Schwarze spent hours on the ice taking notes.

The Cape Crozier rookery, about seventy miles east of McMurdo, is the largest Adélie breeding place in Antarctica. Every year—nobody knows for how long—the birds have returned to this rookery to find their mates, build nests, lay and incubate eggs, and wait for the chicks to hatch and grow.

"All the world loves a penguin," wrote Apsley Cherry-Garrard in *The Worst Journey in the World* in 1922. "I think it is because in many respects they are like ourselves, and in some respects what we should like to be. . . . Their little bodies are so full of curiosity that they have no room for fear. They like mountaineering, and joy-riding on ice-floes; they even like to drill."

The Muller-Schwarzes were less fanciful in their observations. As scientists, they were meticulous about facts, numbers, measurements. All the same, they found their small neighbors entertaining.

The Adélies are so tame that Dietland Muller-Schwarze found it very easy to capture a penguin for observation.

"The birds were so tame," Christine said, "they never seemed to notice we weren't penguins, too. Sometimes they'd peck at us—the way they peck at each other—but it couldn't hurt. Not through all those layers of polar clothing. At the end of six weeks, all of us were walking like penguins."

Every day, as careful observers and honorary penguins, the scientists watched the colony grow. The male birds had arrived first. They waddled around, busily gathering pebbles to build nests, often stealing them from other penguins. Sometimes two or three penguins would fight over a preferred location.

Many of the older penguins were returning to the same neighborhood in which they had nested the previous summer. Earlier biologists had discovered this when they tagged some of the birds, then found them again—year after year—when scientists and birds returned to Cape Crozier.

When the females arrived, a few days later than the males, the noise was deafening. Penguins called to other penguins and somehow found each other in the crowds. Tagged penguins revealed that many pairs had been mated for years. Widows and widowers had to find new mates—or sit alone on empty nests. Young males, building nests for the first time, competed for choice sites. The location of a nest could influence a penguin's success in attracting a mate.

While the penguins were settling in for the summer on the rocky slopes, Christine and Dietland Muller-Schwarze were making themselves at home in a very crowded wooden cabin not far away.

At first they shared the cabin with a young Chilean ornithologist, another biologist, and two American graduate students. Since the four bunks were already occupied, two folding cots were moved in for the newcomers.

"Sometimes it was very bothersome," Christine recalled. "With twenty-four hours of daylight, people were working at all hours. If we were sleeping when somebody came in from the ice, we had to get up and fold our cots to allow them to reach their bunks. And, of course, we couldn't go to bed early if they were still up and working in the cabin."

Every inch of space was used. The four bunks filled one wall. Shelves for equipment and work space occupied the opposite wall. A kerosene stove at the back of the cabin provided heat and melted great quantities of snow in a big boiler. Every day, somebody had to shovel enough snow to fill the boiler to produce all the water needed for drinking, cooking, and washing. All the scientists took turns at this household chore.

An all-purpose table and four chairs completed the furnishings. The table was used for dissecting and preserving specimens or recording notes, as well as for eating and just sitting around and talking.

After two weeks in the crowded cabin, the Muller-Schwarzes were offered private sleeping quarters. One day a helicopter arrived from McMurdo bringing a collapsible fiber glass igloo. When it was set up near the cabin, the two folding beds were moved in.

"There was no room for anything else," Christine remembered. "We could barely squeeze in the two cots. The igloo couldn't be heated at all, so it was very much colder than the cabin. We had to sleep in layers of clothing inside our sleeping bags. When we woke up in the mornings, we'd find icicles hanging from the ceiling, formed from our breathing during the night."

"Day" and "night" are arbitrary terms in Antarctica. Residents set their watches by New Zealand time and try to ignore the eternal daylight of summer or darkness of winter. During the polar summer—November, December, and January—the sun never falls below the horizon. It moves around the sky in a circle that grows smaller and smaller until late December when it shines, almost directly overhead, twenty-four hours a day. Then the circle begins to widen and the sun moves lower in the sky until late March. After a long dusk, it disappears for six months. The Antarctic night ends with the gray-pink dawn of late September.

Emperor penguins (on the ice near McMurdo) are larger than Adélies.

"We sometimes worked until ten or eleven at night," Christine said. "When the weather was good we didn't want to waste any chance to watch the penguins. We were very lucky that summer. The weather was mostly good. We lost only two weeks because of bad weather—and then there were blizzards, with winds up to 120 miles an hour. We couldn't leave the cabin for days at a time."

On a typical good day the two researchers were out on the ice with the penguins. Their particular interest that summer was in the penguin's ability to cope with its enemies—especially the leopard seal. Unlike other seals, which are satisfied to eat fish and krill, the leopards prey on penguins.

Early in the season, when the penguins are swimming toward the rookery, a company of leopard seals will lurk along the shoreline. As the penguins approach—leaping like dolphins out of the water, then diving under the surface—the seals submerge like submarines and go after the unsuspecting birds. This is a dangerous time for the penguins. Some researchers estimate that the seals catch and eat about five percent of the entire breeding population.

Christine and her husband watched this deadly game, determined to be objective scientists even when they found themselves cheering for penguins that escaped and lamenting the ones that were caught.

The leopard seals became a sinister presence. From time to time a great head would rise out of the water with a penguin in its mouth. Then the skuas would circle overhead, waiting for leftovers. These gull-like scavengers pick the bones left by seals. In recent years they have adapted to the presence of humans—especially at McMurdo—by raiding their garbage dumps.

Once on land, Adélie penguins face more danger from skuas than from seals. Adults are seldom attacked, but after the eggs are laid—only two in a nest each season—skuas swoop down on unattended nests to break and eat the eggs. Very few nests are left unguarded. Penguin parents are very protective. Males and females take turns sitting on the eggs for about five weeks, until they hatch. While one partner goes out to sea in search of food, the other incubates the eggs.

When the chicks hatch in early December, both parents—alternately—feed them and guard them from marauding skuas. Sometimes a nest will be attacked by a pair of skuas—one to distract the parent penguin while the other grabs a temporarily unguarded chick. In January, the chicks leave their nests and cluster together in concentrated "day nurseries" while the parents go fishing.

By early February the chicks have lost the brown fluff that covers them during their first two months. Then they are old enough to go to sea themselves—but some of them don't make it as far as the shore. Skuas attack like fighter planes. Only the speediest and luckiest young penguins survive.

These daily dramas in the penguin colony were observed and recorded by the Muller-Schwarze team. They watched through binoculars and recorded with cameras—spending hours on the ice in temperatures that ranged from fifteen above zero (Fahrenheit) to fifteen below.

"It was always cold," Christine recalled, "but I don't think I was ever uncomfortable while working. The clothing provided by NSF was so well-designed. They thought of everything. We wore long thermal underwear with padded windproof pants and insulated boots with woolen socks. Usually we wore a flannel shirt and two sweaters under our parkas."

In many ways, Christine found life at Cape Crozier different from any other she had known, but she adapted quickly. "I think I knew what to expect," she said. "Dietland had told me so much about his experiences in Antarctica."

Five years earlier, Dietland Muller-Schwarze had been the

Adélie penguins at Cape Crozier

first German scientist invited to work with the American research program in Antarctica. At that time he was single, with a brand new Ph.D. from the Max Planck Institute of Behavioral Physiology in Seewiesen, Bavaria. His mentor at the institute had been Konrad Lorenz, the noted zoologist who later received a Nobel Prize.

Soon after his first season with the penguins, Muller-Schwarze returned to Germany and married Christine, a former classmate at Freiburg University. Together the newlyweds set out for the United States, where Dietland was to be an associate professor of wildlife resources at Utah State University.

Christine shared her husband's work from the beginning— hiking with him into the Utah hills to observe the deer, keeping endless records, bringing back several fawns to be cared for at home, almost as part of the family.

"Our penguin studies are only a small part of the work being done all over the world," Christine said. "There are so many different areas of research—and even more researchers."

Some studies are very specialized. A biochemist may analyze penguin proteins or a specific set of glands. Others focus on diving patterns or feeding habits. Paleontologists study fossil penguins to learn more about the evolution of birds in general. Ecologists are interested in the penguin's ability to adapt to the bleak Antarctic environment. A scientist may study a single penguin species—or several.

North Americans and Europeans are inclined to think of penguins as exclusively Antarctic birds. They are not. Some species of penguins are familiar visitors to the beaches of South Australia, New Zealand, South America, and South Africa. Of the estimated eighteen penguin species now living, only four are truly Antarctic. These are probably the most thoroughly scrutinized birds in the world.

When Christine and Dietland Muller-Schwarze began their joint investigation in the austral summer of 1969–70, very little was known about some aspects of penguin behavior. How did the Adélies cope with the predatory skuas and leopard seals? How did more than one species sometimes manage to share a breeding area?

After a second summer with the Adélies at Cape Crozier, the young scientists moved on to the Antarctic Peninsula to get acquainted with other penguins—Chinstraps and Gentoos. During the 1971–72 season, they visited twenty-four rookeries on the peninsula, then boarded the research vessel *Hero* to survey twenty-six more breeding areas on Antarctic islands.

Along with their other work, Christine and her husband began a preliminary census—recording the estimated numbers of each penguin species at each rookery. Later observers were able to use these figures as a baseline for determining whether rookery populations had increased or declined.

During part of that summer, the couple lived on an island shared by three species of penguins—Gentoos, Chinstraps, and Adélies. Meticulous observations by the Muller-Schwarze team later became part of the basic scientific literature now studied by penguin biologists.

The various species, they noticed, were about as different in their habits and preferences as are city dwellers and suburbanites—with variations of opinion about the relative merits of mountains and seashore.

"Gentoo penguins typically nest on low flat areas where their large nests can be widely spaced," they reported. "Chinstrap penguins prefer rocky slopes and the higher elevations. Sometimes Chinstrap penguins practice true cliff nesting. Then, instead of building a complete nest, only a few pebbles (sometimes only five to ten) are deposited on a sloping ledge, preventing the two eggs from rolling down."

The Adélies—true urbanites—built their pebble nests close together on knolls and ridges, similar to the ones at Cape Crozier.

At the end of that season in Antarctica, the Muller-Schwarzes returned to Utah. Soon after the results of their penguin studies were published, they were invited to Syracuse, New York, where Dietland joined the faculty of the College of Environmental Science and Forestry at the State University. He continued the penguin research in Antarctica until 1976, but Christine had new responsibilities at home.

Their first daughter, Annette, was born before they left Utah in 1973. A second daughter, Nina, came along three years later.

"The girls are my main profession now," Christine said. But—

even as a busy mother—she found time to work with her husband, at home and in the field. In the summer of 1977 they shifted their attention from south to north. Continuing the scent-communication work begun in Utah, they went to Sweden and then Labrador to study reindeer.

If Annette and Nina Muller-Schwarze ever visit Antarctica, perhaps they will visit Christine Island, the little penguin colony

Christine Muller-Schwarze with penguin chick

that had no name until their mother's work was honored by U.S. government mapmakers. If one of the daughters should become a polar scientist, she will find no barriers just because she is a woman.

"It's easier for women now," Christine remarked. "The year of my first visit—1969–70—was the turning point. I was very lucky. Because my husband had a grant and I traveled as his assistant, I never had to draft proposals or fill out endless forms as the other women did."

She met one of the other women just before their first trip south. Both were in Washington for the physical checkup necessary to all Antarctic scientists. In the waiting room, Christine talked with Lois Jones, the Ohio geochemist who had organized an all-woman field party to work in the Antarctic dry valleys. Lois' season in Antarctica was a very different story.

Three

PIONEER CAMP: FOR WOMEN ONLY

At the end of a long day of backpacking, pushing against a 40-mile-an-hour wind, Lois Jones slept soundly in the tent she shared with her young assistant, Terry Lee Tickhill. Their two companions, Eileen McSaveney and Kay Lindsay, slept in another tent nearby.

Suddenly Lois found herself wide awake—listening. What for? She didn't quite know. In the Antarctic summer there was no real night, but the women darkened their tents by closing the flaps. After a month in Antarctica, they had managed to adjust to the eternal daylight and slept as well in the filtered green light of the tent as they did in darkness at home.

Sleepily, Lois glanced at her watch. Two-fifteen. Too early to get up and make tea. She shifted around in her sleeping bag, mentally made a checklist for the next day's work, looked at her watch again, and eventually fell asleep.

The next night the same thing happened. She awoke suddenly—listening. Again, her watch told her it was just after 2:00 A.M. When it happened a few more times, she began to feel vaguely disturbed.

37

"I never suffered from insomnia at home," she said. "There was certainly no reason to wake up, tired as I was. One morning at breakfast I mentioned it to the others. It turned out that the same thing had happened to them. All of us had been waking up in the middle of the night—usually about two or two-thirty."

Gradually, the four campers realized what had awakened them. Silence. The sudden absence of a constant background noise they had come to expect. All day and all night they heard the wind—howling, moaning, whistling, hissing, flapping the sides of the tents. They had become so accustomed to it that they hardly noticed it any more—until it stopped.

Twice a day, like the tides, the wind changed direction. At those times, a calm silence closed in and the tents seemed unnaturally still. After ten or fifteen minutes, the wind would start up in the opposite direction, gradually gathering speed until it reached the familiar howl, screech, hiss, and flap.

"You get used to the noise," Lois recalled. "Out in the field, your ears become attuned to certain sounds. Sometimes, when you're waiting for supplies and you don't know when the helicopter will arrive, you go ahead and do your work—but all the time you're listening. Even now, after all these years, I can always hear a helicopter sooner than anybody else."

By December, 1969, Lois, Eileen, Terry, and Kay were beginning to feel at home in the unearthly landscape of the Wright Valley. They learned to cope with daily surprises. Rocks that seemed close enough to reach within minutes turned out to be boulders more than a mile away. The clearest, purest air they had ever breathed played tricks on their judgment of distances. Without dust or smoke to cloud the atmosphere, without buildings or trees to lend perspective, they could judge a mile only by walking that mile.

Crossing a dry valley, on the way to Don Juan Pond, women scientists might be on the moon.

The women had no close neighbors, but they occasionally saw a few New Zealanders who had a year-round camp at the east end of Lake Vanda. Their own small camp consisted of three tiny green tents. Like toy houses in a Monopoly game, the tents were dwarfed by a backdrop of steep rock, rising six thousand feet to meet a vivid blue sky.

"They were very small tents," Lois recalled, "just big enough for two people. Terry and I shared one; Kay and Eileen had another. The third was used for cooking."

The women had placed their tents with great care—only after they had studied the wind patterns. Sleeping tents had to be at right angles to the east or west direction of the wind—and at a safe distance from the cooking tent.

"We were very conscious of fire danger," Lois explained, "so we never had fire at all except in the cooking tent. The

Always aware of fire danger in the dry valleys, the four women scientists placed their sleeping tents away from the cooking tent and at right angles to the wind direction.

air is so dry out there and the wind is so high that if anything ever catches fire it's just *gone*. We had to think what would happen if the cooking tent ever did catch fire. It had to be far enough away from the sleeping tents to keep them out of danger. If our sleeping bags and other gear had burned while we were out in the valley, we'd have been in real trouble. We didn't even use a tarpaulin under our stove—just set it on the bare rock."

Bare rock. No ice or snow. That is still one of the mysteries of the Antarctic dry valleys. When these hidden clearings were first revealed by airborne cameras in 1949, scientists were puzzled. Why, in this ice-covered land, were there ice-free oases? What happened to the snow?

Later investigators, exploring on foot, discovered more wonders in the dry valleys. Pale blue tongues of great glaciers spilled over the tops of mountains surrounding the Wright Valley and crept toward the valley floor. In some places the ice flow stopped abruptly, less than halfway down, cut off by an invisible force that kept it hanging there like a draped curtain.

Snow, if it fell at all, never reached the ground. It didn't melt first and then evaporate. It just disappeared into the dry air.

Among the biggest surprises were the lakes. On a frozen continent, who would expect to find deep lakes, unfrozen in summer? When specialists brought their instruments to measure and analyze the water, they discovered that it was much warmer at the bottom than on the surface. In any ordinary lake the reverse is true: the deeper you go, the colder it gets. Another surprise was the salt in the lakes. Unlike the ice of the freshwater glaciers that fed them, these lakes were salty. The high concentration of salt, scientists said, would absorb and hold the sun's heat, accounting for warmer temperatures in the depths of the lakes—but where did the salt come from? This was one of the mysteries that had brought Lois Jones to Antarctica. Lake Vanda in the Wright Valley was one target of research for Lois and her team.

The mystery of Lake Vanda had attracted Lois' attention a few years earlier when she was a graduate student at the Ohio State University. Geologists at the university's Institute of Polar Studies were doing a great deal of exciting research in Antarctica. One of these men was her advisor, Dr. Gunter Faure.

When Lois asked Faure to help her choose a topic for her Ph.D. dissertation, he mentioned the puzzle of salty lakes in the dry valleys of Antarctica. Nobody had ever really explained them. Here was a challenge for a young geochemist. Lois was fascinated.

"I remember the day he mentioned it to me," Lois said. "I went down to see Colin Bull, the director of the Institute of Polar Studies at that time. Probably more than anyone else at Ohio State, he was responsible for getting our field work under way. I told Colin what I wanted to do and he was very excited about it. Here was somebody at work on a problem he was interested in. We talked for a few minutes. He had his elbows on his desk. Suddenly he stopped talking, looked exasperated, and put his head down on his arms. Then he looked up at me and muttered, 'Sex!'

"I knew what he meant, of course. No woman could expect to do field work in Antarctica. I knew that most men would rather not see women on the Ice, but I could never truly understand it. I wanted to work on the problem anyway, even if I had to do it all in Ohio without ever seeing a dry valley."

Anybody who wanted to work with the U.S. Antarctic Research Program could apply for a grant from the National Science Foundation in Washington, but there was just one way to get to Antarctica. Navy aircraft carried everybody—scientists, technicians, pilots, cooks, and journalists—along with the tons of supplies needed to keep them alive in an icy desert.

Navy men had been first to tame small parts of that desert. They had built the first permanent bases on the continent and had been first to survive the six-month winter night. The Navy had made Antarctica accessible to scientists. Unless the Navy said women could work in Antarctica, women would have to stay at home.

Lois stayed in Ohio, but she went ahead with her polar project. She planned the research, worked out a formula, and began looking around for geologists who might have rock samples from the area she wanted to study.

"I was lucky," she said. "Dr. Derry Koob had worked in the dry valleys during the previous season and had collected excellent depth profiles from two lakes, Bonney and Vanda. He was very gracious and gave me enough samples to get started on my dissertation."

It was a good start, but Lois needed more than leftover rocks from the research of other scientists. Without bedrock samples and rocks from the river that flows into Lake Vanda, her calculations would be incomplete. If only she could go to Antarctica—but that was impossible. Lois had to find somebody—a man—to do field work especially for her project.

"We had a graduate student from France," she recalled. "Raymond Montigny, who was working with Dr. Faure that year, was eager to go to Antarctica. NSF gave him a small grant to go down and collect samples for me. He was enthusiastic, but he ran into problems. He couldn't get to some of the areas

Lois Jones calls this a portrait of herself and the wind.

where I wanted him to collect samples. I had asked for drilling that couldn't be done.

"He tried. But some of the things I had asked were impossible. The situation in the field could be very different from what I imagined, sitting in my office. You have to do a lot of improvising in the field. Questions kept popping up—as they do in any research—and I wondered if I could ever answer them without doing my own field work."

She managed. With half a world between herself and her subject, she completed an original research project and earned a Ph.D. *Then* she learned that maybe women were going to be allowed to work in Antarctica after all.

"The word was getting around that a lot of qualified women were applying for grants to do research in Antarctica," she recalled. "I was told, very tentatively, that if I wanted to submit

Kay Lindsay during Survival School

Eileen McSaveney at Survival School

Terry Lee Tickhill collects a water sample from Canopus Pond.

a research proposal to NSF, the Navy just might be willing to give it a try."

Lois worked out a detailed proposal for ten weeks of research—suggesting goals, methods, supplies, and budget. Final approval did not come at once, but she was told to select two other women to work with her in the field. Eileen McSaveney, then a graduate student in geology, was her first choice. An undergraduate, who later was to change her mind, was asked to go along as field assistant.

"We thought we had a chance," Lois said, "but we didn't want to be too optimistic. We weren't really sure until June, 1969. Then we learned that our proposal had been approved and the Navy had agreed to take four women instead of three."

Kay Lindsay, the wife of a geologist in the department, seemed a likely fourth. Her husband, John, had been to the Antarctic several times. Lois felt that Kay would be realistic about the kind of living conditions they could expect. Although her scientific training had been in entomology, Kay was eager to join the geology team.

Meanwhile, during all the off-again, on-again uncertainty about the expedition, the young field assistant accepted another job and left the team. Lois looked around for a replacement.

"That's when we found Terry," Lois recalled. "Terry Lee Tickhill was only nineteen—a sophomore majoring in chemistry—but she turned out to be a careful, meticulous scientist. I've never had another field assistant like Terry—before or since that trip. She seemed to know what I had in my mind. When we were working in the field and I wanted something and turned to her to ask, she already had it ready. It was very easy working with Terry."

Ten years later, Terry said the experience had deeply affected her life and career. Now an aquatic ecologist with the U.S. Fish and Wildlife Service and the wife of a marine biologist, Dr. Terry Terrell says she might never have finished college at all if she had not signed up for that trip to Antarctica.

"I was majoring in chemistry," she recalled, "but I knew I didn't want to spend my life in a lab. I didn't really know what I wanted to do. The Antarctic trip seemed a good opportunity to sort out my thoughts. It was a lot more than that. It was a year of phenomenal discovery for me—and some good, solid scientific work as well."

Their scientific work began before the women left Ohio, but all four were impatient to explore their frozen laboratory. They studied maps and checked lists of equipment—and learned to cope with reporters. Persistent requests for interviews and the constant ringing of telephones took up more and more time.

Lois was disillusioned when she saw some of the newspaper stories. Appearing under headlines like POWDERPUFF EX- PLORERS TO INVADE SOUTH POLE, the stories seemed to her trivial, frivolous, having nothing to do with the work they were doing.

"Some of the reporters asked such silly questions," she re- called with some irritation. "They asked, 'Will you wear lipstick while you work?' and 'How will you have your hair done?' Can you imagine a male scientist answering a question like that? They weren't *all* that silly. Walter Sullivan of *The New York Times* wrote the best story of all. He seemed really interested in our work and explained what we were trying to do."

Suddenly the suspense was over. The Navy approved their travel and the four women flew to Washington. At Andrews Air Force Base, near the capital, they boarded a military plane for the first leg of their flight to the bottom of the world. In

Christchurch, New Zealand, they were outfitted with polar clothing and were followed everywhere by more photographers and reporters. There was no escape, even aboard the plane that carried them to McMurdo.

Dreams of a quiet, isolated camp on the ice grew more and more attractive. At McMurdo, the women found still more reporters. Lois was thoroughly sick of publicity, but there was one more media event to endure. She and her team were to become the first women to reach the South Pole.

"It wasn't supposed to be such a production," she remembered. "We weren't even scheduled to go to the Pole—but we had a few days in McMurdo and I asked the NSF representative if I could ride down to the Pole on one of the supply planes—if there were space."

During the summer season in Antarctica, the big ski-equipped Hercules aircraft make as many flights to the Pole as they can. They carry extra supplies to be stored for winter when no planes can get in. Normally, the planes don't stay long. They leave their engines running while they unload, then fly right back to McMurdo. Lois saw a chance to get an overall view of the geology of the area where she and her companions would be working.

"Geology is so nice down there," she said. "When you fly over bare rock you can see the whole panorama of the rock sequence—you're not hampered by trees or soil. All I expected to do was to ride down and back with the plane, to press my nose against the window and look. I was totally surprised when it turned out to be a big operation."

By that time there were seven women on the Antarctic continent. At McMurdo, Lois, Eileen, Kay, and Terry were joined by Pam Young, a New Zealand biologist, and Jean Pearson, a reporter for the *Detroit Free Press*. At Cape Crozier, Christine Muller-Schwarze had already settled in, a few weeks earlier, to work with her husband among the penguins.

The Navy was very careful not to show favoritism. All seven women were invited to be *first* at the Pole. Christine declined the invitation, saying she didn't want to interrupt her research, but the other six were flown to the Amundsen-Scott base at the Pole, just for a day. Their landing was carefully staged, with photographers in mind.

"The Navy wanted to make sure that no single woman could claim to be ahead of the others," Lois said. "We thought we could just sneak out of the plane, one at a time, and nobody would ever know who was first. But the Navy had it all worked out."

Once the plane landed, the women were instructed to wait. A huge cargo ramp was lowered from the belly of the plane and the bay doors opened wide. Then, with cameras clicking, the six women marched down the ramp, arm-in-arm, and stepped simultaneously onto the ice.

Every step was recorded. At the symbolic, mirror-topped "Pole," the women were photographed shaking hands with the admiral. On a guided tour of the base they were followed by cameras. After lunch and a little conversation with the men stationed at the Pole, they boarded the supply plane again and returned to McMurdo.

A few days later, at last, the Ohio team was far away from reporters and photographers. A Navy helicopter delivered the women and their gear to their first camp—in the dry, boulder-strewn Taylor Valley. Now they could start doing the work they had come to do.

For the first three weeks of their ten-week season, their home

In the Taylor Valley the geologists found the first flowing water they had seen in Antarctica—a meltwater stream from the Rhone Glacier—on a particularly warm day.

was a little A-frame house near Lake Bonney. Built for the use of earlier research teams, the house was relatively well equipped with a large stove, a generator, ceiling lights, and camp beds.

"It was cold as sin," Lois recalled, "much colder than the tents we lived in later. But it was great to be out there where we could set our own schedule, free from interruptions. Jean Pearson came for a few days, to write a story for her paper. She was a big help—really pitched in and worked with us. She stayed longer than she had planned. One of the helicopters crashed and they were unable to come and pick her up."

If those first weeks were a test period, the women felt they

Eileen McSaveney and Terry Lee Tickhill examine a weathered boulder. They called it "the people-eating mushroom."

had passed the test. Ominous forecasts of "hairpulling and tears" proved false.

"We got along much better, I think, than most groups isolated like that," Dr. Jones recalled. "I'm not saying it was all sweet harmony. Sometimes *little* things would get on our nerves.

"For example, one girl had a way of stirring her tea—and stirring, and *stirring*, and STIRRING! I began to dread that 'tinkle, tinkle, tinkle' in the cold silence at every single meal. I wondered if the others were bothered by it. One day, I heard myself yelling, 'For heaven's sake, stop *stirring!*' Then I hated myself for being so touchy. The others confessed that they had been irritated by it, too, but had hesitated to say anything. The girl hadn't realized she was doing it—so after that she didn't stir quite so much."

When the first segment of their research was completed, the

women were picked up by a helicopter and returned to McMurdo. There was time for a shower and shampoo and a little talk about what was going on in the rest of the world—but they were impatient to be off again.

"We had stopped caring what was going on in the rest of the world," Lois said. "I think our attitude was fairly common. When you first arrive at McMurdo, you still care. I remember how we used to hurry down to the cafeteria at breakfast time, to pick up one of the little mimeographed sheets that served as the local newspaper. For a while, everybody grabbed one and the supply soon disappeared—but after a few days there were stacks left over, even if we were late for breakfast. Nobody really cared any more. Everything there is directed toward one thing—getting science done. You resent the intrusion of all those other things."

There were no more intrusions after the women set up their tent camp in the windy Wright Valley. For the next two months they had no time to be bored. During days filled with sampling, measuring, testing, and recording, they were too busy, even, to remember that they were on trial. By the time the season was over, everybody seemed to have forgotten the controversy that had surrounded the admission of the first women to the Antarctic laboratory.

Lois, Eileen, Kay, and Terry returned to Ohio to analyze their findings and publish them. Fellow scientists congratulated them. Nobody said, "Good work—for a bunch of women." Ten years later, Lois Jones still felt proud of her teammates and the work they did that year.

"I feel that women are greatly suited to polar environments—perhaps more so than men," she said. "Some men come back from the field with their skin dry—often cracked and bleeding.

We never had that problem. Women may not have the physical strength of men, but given some insight into a situation, they can get the job done.''

The success of their pioneer season on the ice made it easier for women scientists who came later. Still, Lois believes that the struggle for equality is not over.

''Even today,'' she said, ''young women scientists who are getting their careers started have not only the same difficulties as young men, but the additional problems of 'type casting.' It is still true that for a woman to be respected in a given job, she has to do it better than a man.''

Four

SEAGOING SCIENTISTS

Like Captain Cook, Mary Alice McWhinnie sailed around in Antarctic waters for years without seeing Antarctica. Unlike the famous British explorer, she eventually landed on the continent and worked there, year after year. She even became the first woman ever to head an Antarctic research station.

For ten years her southern laboratory was a floating one, aboard the research ship USNS *Eltanin*. Between 1962 and 1972, Dr. McWhinnie spent almost every austral summer at sea. She was studying krill, tiny shrimplike creatures that may one day feed hungry people.

At the time of her death in 1980, Dr. McWhinnie was an international authority on krill. Probably nobody else in the world knew as much about krill as did Mary Alice McWhinnie and her young colleague, Charlene Denys.

"Very few students have the kind of opportunities I had," Charlene commented. "Very few students live and work with their advisors, four months out of the year, in a setting as remote as Antarctica. I started out as her student and became her assistant, but she trained me to be her colleague. We also became good friends."

Seagoing biologist Mary Alice McWhinnie

The focus of Dr. McWhinnie's research for nearly twenty years, the krill, a small animal no more than two inches long, is vitally important to almost every other creature in the Antarctic oceans. Krill are the bread and meat of the whole food chain. Whales eat more than a million tons of the little crustaceans every year. Seals, penguins, skuas, fish, and squid also consume their share.

In recent years, many nutritionists have begun to think of krill as valuable food for humans, too. Krill are rich in protein and contain all the essential amino acids. And they're relatively easy to catch. Krill have a habit of "swarming" in huge numbers near the ocean surface. Scientists call it an "aggregation," since krill don't actually *swarm* in a particular pattern. Whatever it is—aggregation or swarm—fishermen can see the krill from a distance as a reddish patch on the water that may be two hundred feet across, or even larger. One West German trawler netted thirty-five tons of krill in eight minutes.

As early as 1977 in some countries, krill turned up in supermarkets as soup, paste, meal, breaded krill sticks, or simply frozen packages of krill. In Japan, the USSR, Poland, West Germany, Chile, Korea, and Taiwan, krill became a profitable commercial crop. In the United States, some krill was used in pet foods, but many food packagers were still cautious.

A few years ago, during a summer at Palmer Station, Mary Alice McWhinnie and Charlene Denys cooked a batch of krill in their laboratory, just to see how it would taste.

"It tastes like bland shrimp," Charlene said. "Mary Alice wasn't enthusiastic about it, but I wanted to try again—in a real kitchen, with butter and garlic and maybe a little breading. Later I did that—in my sister's kitchen in Madison, Wisconsin. We had a small dinner party with krill as the main course. Everybody said they were delicious."

Everywhere they went, the two scientists were questioned about the commercial uses of krill, but their main concern has been with fundamental questions about the biology of krill. They wanted to learn what the tiny animals are made of, how fast they grow and reproduce, what they eat, how they see, how often they spawn.

When the first tentative attempts were made to exploit krill as food for humans, krill biologists around the world were wary.

"Wait a minute," they said, in effect. "If we harvest krill on a large scale, what will happen to the rest of the animals that depend on krill for food?" Dr. McWhinnie decided to do something about the questions in her mind.

"We know what happened to the whales a hundred years ago," she said. "As soon as the vast resources of the Antarctic became known, man went down and decimated the whales and seals. Now, with protection, maybe the whales are coming back. But whales eat a lot of krill. All Antarctic sea creatures depend on krill—directly or indirectly. So, if we begin to harvest krill for human consumption, we'll reduce the source of food for these other animals. Before we risk irreparable damage to the Antarctic ecosystem, we have to find out if there is enough to go around."

At a London meeting in 1977, scientists from fifteen Antarctic Treaty nations heard Mary Alice McWhinnie propose an international effort to conserve krill—"the world's last great untapped food source." The first step in that effort, she suggested, should be an extensive study of the biology of krill.

The audience saw a small, slim woman with light-brown hair and direct blue eyes. Her clear, midwestern voice carried to the back of the room and the scientists listened. A few days later, Mary Alice McWhinnie was already at work on her part of the study.

Her intense curiosity about the world around her, especially living things, began some fifty years earlier in Elmhurst, Illinois. As a child she liked to help her father work in the family garden.

"I used to pick the worms off the tomato plants," she recalled. "My sisters wouldn't touch them, so the job was mine. I thought they were interesting. I had to learn to tell one kind of worm from another because I had to be very careful about the ones Dad used for fishing."

Sometimes Mary Alice went along with her father when he fished, especially in the summers when the family went to a Wisconsin lake for vacations. They kept a small rowboat tied up outside their cottage and Mary Alice learned to row.

Years later, aboard the 4000-ton *Eltanin*, Dr. McWhinnie often thought of those fishing excursions with her father. His little rowboat was the first of several boats and ships that would play an important part in her life. The questions she asked about the fish in Wisconsin would lead her, eventually, into a life of marine research.

After graduation from high school, Mary Alice earned her bachelor's and master's degrees in biology from DePaul University in Chicago. She transferred to Northwestern for a Ph.D., then returned to DePaul as a teacher. Chicago became her permanent home.

The thought of being a polar biologist didn't enter her mind—until one cold Chicago winter. In was 1958. In her laboratory at DePaul, Dr. McWhinnie was at work on a problem involving crayfish—how fast they grow and how often they shed their shells. While repeating some experiments she had done the previous summer she ran into trouble. For some reason, the experiments wouldn't work at all.

"I couldn't figure out what was wrong," she said. "The crayfish stopped growing and molting. Nothing seemed to work the way it had in the earlier experiments. Then I realized that the tap water in Chicago was awfully cold that time of year. It was about two degrees above freezing. Maybe that had something to do with the problem. So I took the animals out of the cold water, kept them at room temperature, and they started behaving exactly as they had done before in the summer experiments.

"I said to myself, 'That's it! They don't like the cold.' So I tried various temperatures and discovered their limit was eight degrees Centigrade. Below that, they simply stopped their normal processes."

Dr. McWhinnie was aware that her American crayfish had distant relatives in the Antarctic. These creatures thrive in oceans much colder than Chicago's tap water. Earlier scientists, studying Antarctic whales, had seen the giant mammals feeding on huge swarms of krill—even at the edge of the ice pack. Krill, like crayfish, are crustaceans.

"I knew that krill live in water that ranges from minus two to plus one degree, Centigrade, and they don't seem to mind," Dr. McWhinnie said. "They keep on molting and growing in the cold. I wanted to know why they could live in icy water and my crayfish couldn't. Suddenly, I wanted to go to the Antarctic to study krill—to see what kind of biochemical tricks they had to play around with."

Knowing that the National Science Foundation was then involved in all kinds of Antarctic research, she worked out a proposal in 1959 and sent it off. Her customary signature, "M. A. McWhinnie," gave no clue to her sex.

At the NSF offices in Washington, those who read her proposal were interested. This Chicago biologist deserved encouragement. A letter was sent to "M. A. McWhinnie"—describing facilities at McMurdo and outlining the procedure scientists should follow when applying for NSF support.

"When I read about the accommodations at McMurdo—at that time a barracks for thirty men—I realized that the people at NSF didn't know I was a woman. So I just forgot about it."

Nobody could accuse Dr. McWhinnie of pushing her way into the previously all-male world of Antarctic science. She simply set aside the idea—until a representative of the National Science Foundation came to her office, about six months later.

Her visitor from Washington, Dr. Morton D. Turner from the NSF Office of Polar Programs, wanted to know why she hadn't followed up her earlier proposal for studying krill in the Antarctic. Did she think women were excluded from the U.S. Antarctic Research Program? It was true that women did not yet work on the continent, but that would surely change. They talked about the work she was doing and what she hoped to do.

A short time later she heard from Dr. George A. Llano, then chief scientist for the NSF polar biology programs. Would Dr. McWhinnie like to cruise to the Antarctic? The NSF had just acquired a new research ship with well-equipped labs and comfortable cabins. From the decks of the *Eltanin,* she could collect her krill and study them on the spot.

When the *Eltanin* sailed south from Valparaiso, Chile, in October, 1962, Mary Alice McWhinnie was aboard. It was the first in a remarkable series of cruises that brought highly organized science, for the first time, to the southern oceans.

"*Eltanin* was an ideal research ship," Dr. McWhinnie recalled. "I knew that ship for more than ten years—worked on board during six seasons. By the time I left the ship in February, 1972, it had the best marine research program in the world. For the first time, marine programs were interacting—exchanging data—studying the entire water column."

After her first cruise aboard *Eltanin,* Mary Alice McWhinnie returned to the shipboard laboratory in 1965, 1967, 1969, and 1970. Two years later, when the ship headed for McMurdo, Dr. McWhinnie was the *Eltanin*'s chief scientist.

The headline in a Chicago newspaper was startling. As Dr.

McWhinnie remembered it, the story proclaimed: DR. MARY ALICE McWHINNIE TAKES SHIP TO SOUTH POLE.

"I nearly dropped dead when I saw that!" Dr. McWhinnie laughed. "Take a four-thousand-ton ship to the center of a continent? That's a job I'm not quite equal to!"

Except for confused geography, the story was essentially true. She did take the ship to McMurdo—not to the Pole, some eight hundred miles inland. Sailing from Lyttelton Harbor, near Christchurch, New Zealand, on January 17, 1972, *Eltanin* headed south for forty days and 4505 nautical miles. Along the way the ship made scheduled stops to allow the twenty-six scientists and their assistants to take measurements and collect specimens and water samples.

As chief scientist, Dr. McWhinnie was responsible for turning over the ship to a group of geologists who were waiting at McMurdo. After ten years as a polar biologist, she would at last set foot on the Antarctic continent.

Eltanin reached McMurdo on schedule, February 25, 1972. Dr. McWhinnie's first visit to the station was a brief one, just a few days while waiting for a plane to take her to New Zealand. Two years later she would stay much longer—and then she would command a very different research vessel.

Its name was *Riff Raft.* Dr. McWhinnie christened it herself, cracking a bottle of California wine against its plywood deck as it slid into the icy water of McMurdo Sound. The twelve-foot square raft had a steel frame and was kept afloat by eight 55-gallon oil drums welded together. A 42-inch hole in the middle of the deck made it possible to lower nets and buckets into the water and haul up specimens of sea life.

Three research assistants in wet suits were the full crew. *Riff Raft* was not an ocean-going vessel but it did venture into the

Fishing through the ice, Dr. McWhinnie, Sr. Mary Odile Cahoon, and colleague D. Schenborn haul up the day's catch.

Sound, always safely attached to land by means of a steel cable controlled by a power winch mounted on a truck.

That year of 1974, Dr. McWhinnie was the station scientific leader at McMurdo, the first woman ever to hold that post. Another woman biologist, Sister Mary Odile Cahoon, a teaching nun from St. Scholastica College in Duluth, Minnesota, worked with her.

"It was understood," Dr. McWhinnie explained, "that one of my assistants would be a woman. At that time, no woman principal investigator could go alone. I had known Sister Odile when she was a student in our department at DePaul. Now

she had a Ph.D. from Toronto and was teaching in Duluth—
so I invited her to join our team at McMurdo."

Sister Odile accepted. Later, she recalled no particular surprise
at being chosen to accompany her friend and former teacher
to Antarctica for the winter.

"I had never even thought of polar research until Mary Alice
asked me to go with her for the winter, but I knew about her

In winter, two scientists do their share of waiting on tables in the mess hall.

work—knew she wanted to spend a winter there. I was very
pleased to work with her again. At the time, I didn't really
think about how unusual it would be to be working at the
bottom of the world—two women in a community of young
men."

With à little mischief in her voice, Sister Odile described

herself and her colleague as two "maiden aunts." "It wasn't surprising that Mary Alice would look for a mature assistant," she said. "Both the Navy and NSF were still a little uptight about having women at McMurdo for the winter. Let's be honest—for such a long period of isolation, I'm sure they felt more comfortable having a couple of maiden aunts test the situation."

The two women arrived in January, at the height of the austral summer, when McMurdo was a bustling community of nearly a thousand people. After the last plane flew out at the end of February, only a handful of "winter-overs" were left—128 men and two women. Mary Alice McWhinnie and Sister Odile Cahoon became the first women ever to spend a winter at McMurdo.

"We were there especially for studies in winter biology," Dr. McWhinnie said. "As in other sciences, the seasons are distinct. Most of my krill studies had been done during the austral summer, so it was important to find out what happened to the animals in winter. We knew we would be cut off from the rest of the world for a while."

Winter began officially on April 24. The small band of scientists and technicians at McMurdo watched the sun go down at 12:45 P.M., knowing it wouldn't rise again until August. There would be no more mail from home, no fresh fruit and vegetables from New Zealand, no planes or ships bringing news from outside. Except for their radio links—including conversations with ham radio operators in various countries—they were completely isolated.

"You can't really overcome the feeling of isolation," Sister Odile recalled. "When you see that last plane go out in February, you know there won't be another one until September. Mary Alice and I were too busy to let it bother us much, but it was worse for some of the military men. Some of them had to be there just for the opening of the station. Then—after they had done what they had to do and there was nothing more—boredom set in. They felt imprisoned."

The handful of people who remained at McMurdo during the winter were occupying a station that was, officially, "closed." Every summer, usually in September, there is an official opening when new scientists arrive for the season and the population grows to nearly a thousand.

Sister Odile, an avid outdoorswoman from Minnesota, loved the rugged life in Antarctica. Before the sun set for the winter,

Sr. Odile cuts the cake, while Dr. McWhinnie looks on.

she explored the area around McMurdo, climbing into ice caves and lowering herself by rope into crevasses. Now she laughs when people ask her if she wore a nun's habit in the Antarctic. ("Lumberjack shirt and jeans, like everybody else," she said.) The only clue to her profession was a ring she wore, a symbol of her religious order.

"People did bring their problems to us," she said. "They would drop into the lab and talk. But no more to me than to Mary Alice. Both of us were their maiden aunts."

As the station scientific leader, Dr. McWhinnie had plenty to do. In addition to her own research, she was responsible for keeping the whole scientific operation running smoothly. For one thing, she had to make sure that everybody understood the importance of safety precautions—particularly the observance of weather-condition signals.

"There are three signals," she explained. "Green, yellow, and red lights are used to indicate three kinds of weather conditions:

"When the light is green—Condition Three—you know the weather is good. You can go anywhere you like—within the base. There is a general rule that *nobody* goes outside the base, anytime, without another person. And you must call headquarters before leaving.

"A yellow light—Condition Two—means the weather is not too bad to get around in—but you must call before you leave your building and mustn't go out without another person.

"A red light—Condition One—means the weather is really bad. Don't leave the building. Just stay where you are. All buildings at McMurdo are stocked with extra food and clothing—and of course we all have radios and telephones."

The winter started routinely. Dr. McWhinnie usually worked most of the night in her laboratory—as she had in Chicago—with a pot of coffee at her elbow.

"I don't need much sleep," she insisted. "I guess I'm a nocturnal beast. When I was department chairman at DePaul I used to work until I could hear the birds chirping. At McMurdo there weren't any birds, but I usually managed to quit in time to get a few hours' sleep before returning to the lab at nine-thirty or ten every morning."

Each night, while she worked, Dr. McWhinnie knew she could count on one visitor. Greg Nickell, the young biology lab manager, usually dropped in to check supplies and ask if she needed anything. He was taking guitar lessons and sometimes sat at one end of the lab and practiced his music.

"Sometimes he'd just drop in and talk for a while—about all sorts of things. He had a bachelor's degree from the University of Nevada and wanted to go back for a master's in desert biology. He was full of questions about my research—just interested in *everything*."

One morning, Dr. McWhinnie recalls, there were a number of telephone calls for Greg from people who wanted to ask about supplies. She realized that she hadn't seen him since about ten-fifteen the previous night when he had left the lab to go to a guitar lesson.

"When he didn't show up for lunch, I began to be alarmed. Greg hadn't missed lunch since I'd known him. I called the machine shop and the supply office and the personnel building. Nobody had seen him. Then I remembered the trucks. He often had to deliver supplies to various labs and used one of the trucks. His favorite was a new Dodge truck known as Number 588. I didn't want to alarm everybody on the base, but I knew I had to ask for a search-and-rescue team to look for 588."

Sixteen hours later, the team found 588 at the bottom of a 600-foot drop off the road to Scott Base. Greg's frozen body was found sixty feet away.

"It was a sad winter for all of us," Dr. McWhinnie remembers. "The accident happened in May. There was no way anybody could leave McMurdo before September—so we just had to get on with our work."

The isolated researchers—including two exchange scientists from Poland and the USSR—endured three more sunless months of blizzards and bitter cold. A July storm destroyed the radio shack and damaged other buildings when winds reached 125 miles an hour. In early August the sun was still invisible, but the sky had begun to lighten—a pink-and-gray dawn.

On the second of September, an expectant group gathered at Williams Field on the Ross Ice Shelf to watch for the first planes of the new season. The temperature was forty-two degrees below zero, but the watchers were in a festive mood, like children waiting for a parade to begin.

Right on schedule, two big Hercules aircraft appeared on the horizon, circled, and landed. It was an annual celebration. The planes brought two tons of mail and plenty of fresh fruit, milk, and vegetables—the first since February. They also delivered thirty scientists, ready for an early start on research projects.

As soon as the planes refueled they were ready to take off again. Mary Alice McWhinnie was aboard the first return flight. She had survived an exhausting winter, but there was no time for a holiday—yet. She was already overdue in Chicago where fall classes at DePaul were about to begin.

When she walked into her laboratory, a few days later, she found a young woman waiting to see her. Charlene Denys had just enrolled at DePaul as a Ph.D. student in biology. Before the year was over, Dr. McWhinnie had a new assistant and Charlene had discovered a totally unexpected new career.

"I knew that Dr. McWhinnie did research in Antarctica," Charlene said, "but it never occurred to me that I might work

Approaching the Antarctic Peninsula aboard the research ship Hero

there too. One day she walked in and asked me, 'Have you ever thought of going to Antarctica?' I honestly had not, and I said so. 'Well,' she said, 'think about it.' So I thought about it—and suddenly I was fascinated. I told her I would like to go."

Just before Christmas in 1975, the two Chicago women flew to Argentina, the first leg of their journey south. At Ushuaia, a small port in Tierra del Fuego, they boarded the ship that would take them the rest of the way. Dr. McWhinnie was not going back to McMurdo but to another part of Antarctica— the Antarctic Peninsula. "The banana belt," it was called by McMurdo regulars, because the weather was not so cold. It wasn't exactly balmy, as Jennie Darlington had discovered nearly thirty years earlier, but above freezing in summer.

For Charlene Denys, the voyage from Tierra del Fuego was an adventure she would never forget. During the next few years it would become a familiar route, but now it was all new. She watched the rugged mountains disappear—as Darwin had done more than a century earlier. Then she explored the ship.

R/V Hero, named for the tiny sloop commanded by Captain Nathaniel Palmer when he discovered the Antarctic Peninsula, was built in 1968, specifically for Antarctic research. *Hero* is much smaller than the *Eltanin*—about one-sixth as large—but it also has laboratory space and sophisticated equipment. On a typical cruise, the small wooden steamer carries a crew of twelve and eight scientists.

Every austral summer, December through March, *Hero* carries a variety of research teams—geologists, oceanographers, marine biologists—to and from Palmer Station on Anvers Island. Unlike McMurdo—a big city, by comparison—Palmer Station has a total population of about forty people in summer and no more than ten in winter. Since there is no permanent landing strip for aircraft, almost everybody arrives by ship. In addition to *Hero,* there are often other ships in port—commercial fishing vessels and even a few cruise ships.

For Mary Alice McWhinnie, *Hero* was the fourth and last of a series of boats that influenced her life. The first had been her father's rowboat on a Wisconsin lake. Then came *Eltanin* and the makeshift *Riff Raft.* During the last years of her life, *Hero* and Palmer Station became her second home.

With the enthusiasm of a housewife decorating a summer cottage, she rearranged the laboratory at Palmer to suit her research. When she designed a large aquarium, with sea water constantly flowing through, she made it possible to keep krill alive in the laboratory.

When Charlene Denys wanted to study krill vision and the bioluminescence of the animals, which glow in the dark like

Charlene Denys, student and later colleague of Mary Alice McWhinnie, is photographed with feathered friend.

fireflies, the two women worked out a system to control the amount of light in the aquarium. Within a few seasons, they had discovered details about the biology of krill that nobody had known before. They learned that the average krill lifespan is more than two years, that krill grow new exoskeletons at regular intervals—even if they haven't outgrown the old ones— and they have an unpleasant habit of eating each other if they can't find other food.

Each year, Charlene accepted more responsibility for the work at Palmer. "My right hand," Dr. McWhinnie called her. Then, without warning, Charlene found herself in charge of the program.

The DePaul scientists were preparing for the 1979–80 season when Dr. McWhinnie was struck down by an illness that left her paralyzed and unable to speak.

Charlene carried on the work at Palmer that year. She supervised a technician, advised a graduate student at work on a master's degree, completed her own Ph.D. project, and still found time to greet a shipload of Chilean tourists.

In March, when the season was almost over, she received a dreaded message from Chicago. After more than half a year of illness, Dr. McWhinnie was dead.

It was a sad homecoming for the DePaul team when they returned to Chicago. For Charlene it meant new responsibilities and decisions. The whole krill project, supported by NSF through a grant to Mary Alice McWhinnie, was now officially without support.

"Mary Alice spent a lot of time training me to be a professional," Charlene said. "She wanted me to be able to write proposals and to prepare data for publication. I learned how to do it, but never dreamed I would have to do it so soon."

NSF provided a special grant for Charlene to remain at DePaul for another year to assemble the masses of scientific data gathered by the McWhinnie team in Antarctica and to prepare it for publication. While she completed the work begun by her mentor nearly twenty years earlier, other women were beginning new research projects in Antarctica. Some of them would work at Palmer Station in the Mary Alice McWhinnie Biology Center, re-named during the 1980–81 season to honor the seagoing scientist.

Five

SIGNALS
FROM LONGWIRE

Nothing seemed more urgent to Irene Peden—at first—than mastering the rickety ladder at Longwire Station. After waiting five years to see the area where her experiments were being done, she had traveled thousands of miles from Seattle. Now, for a few uncertain minutes, radio science would have to wait until she could climb down that ladder.

She was directing a series of experiments involving Very Low Frequency radio signals for the University of Washington where she was an associate professor of electrical engineering. In November, 1970, her field laboratory was a tiny outpost under the ice, about fifteen miles from the older and larger Byrd Station. Its formal name was Byrd VLF Substation, but everybody called it "Longwire" because of its principal piece of equipment, a 21-mile-long antenna.

"I'll never forget my first glimpse of Longwire," Irene recalled. "As we approached, by very slow trackmaster, we could see nothing at all on the horizon except for a little haze above an absolutely flat expanse of snow and ice. Suddenly, there was a communications antenna ahead—and a flag—but no visible buildings."

The little substation, made up of three trailer vans, had been set up on the surface five years earlier. Gradually, under snow that drifted and piled up, it disappeared from view. Now it was frozen under the ice.

"As we came closer," she said, "we could see a few little protrusions—including a small plastic dome—but where was the entrance? Then I saw an open hatchway and a sort of jerry-built ladder. That was the front door of our new home."

Shivering a little at the recollection, Dr. Peden described the perilous entrance to Longwire Station:

"The top of the ladder leaned toward a slippery thirty-degree slope—just too far away for an easy step. There was nothing to hang onto. You just had to try to balance your right foot on the icy slope, put your left foot on the top rung of the

Julia Vickers helps Irene Peden get started down the ladder to Longwire Station, 24 feet under the ice.

ladder, then shift your weight. I looked at the ladder, then down at my bunny boots and padded pants, and was sure I'd never make it.''

Heavy layers of polar clothing made Irene feel clumsy as she jumped off the tractor. "I felt like a snowman," she said, "with my arms sticking out at the sides. When you're wearing inflated boots and several pairs of socks, it's an effort just to pick up your feet—to put one foot in front of the other. I knew I couldn't possibly have enough co-ordination and strength to get down that ladder.''

The structure had been put together very casually. Every year,

"After a couple of round trips, I knew I could do it."

as the station sank lower and lower into the ice, somebody would add another rung or two to the ladder.

"And the somebodies," Dr. Peden noted, "were all in their twenties. Male—with long legs. They did not build that ladder for a short female wearing padded pants and bunny boots. But, you do what you have to do. I gritted my teeth, planted my right foot on the slope, swung the left—and I made it!"

Later that night, Irene Peden lay awake in her bunk and worried about the ladder. Here she was at the bottom of the world—at last! It hadn't been easy to get here. For five years she had worked on the project by remote control from Seattle. Even though she was a principal investigator, she had not been allowed to set up her own experiments on the ice or to do her own measuring and testing. Because she was a woman, male graduate students had been sent to do that for her.

Now, with the support of the National Science Foundation, she was actually here. Some of her equipment had been lost, enroute from New Zealand, but in spite of the handicap she was determined to succeed. Plenty to do! No time to waste in worrying about a silly ladder.

After what seemed like several sleepless hours, Irene made up her mind. In the tiny room she shared with Julia Vickers, everything was quiet. In the upper bunk, Julia lay still, breathing regularly. As quietly as she could, Irene climbed out of her bunk and struggled into all those layers of long johns, padded pants, sweaters, parka, socks, and boots. Moving silently through the tunnel to the bottom of the ladder, she looked up through the open hatch.

Daylight! Maybe it was later than she had thought. Then she remembered where she was. In the Antarctic summer, there was always daylight.

Quickly—hoping the others were still asleep—she stepped onto the bottom rung and climbed the ladder.

"I stood out there on the surface for a few minutes and looked around. Then I took a deep breath, reached for the top rung, and climbed back down. After a couple of round trips, I knew I could do it."

When the others came into the little mess hall for breakfast they could smell coffee. Their leader was sitting there, fully dressed, ready to start the day's work.

The project had been planned in Seattle long before Irene and her team landed at Longwire. She and her co-workers at the University of Washington were trying to answer some fundamental questions about the behavior of radio waves. What happened to these waves when they traveled through mile-thick layers of polar ice?

At that time, very little was known about the electromagnetic properties of the deeper ice. Glaciologists had learned how deep the ice was by sending sonar explosions and measured sound waves down through it. They measured the time it took for the signals to travel down and back, reflected from the rocky surface underneath. These measurements revealed that the ice was as deep as seven thousand feet in some places. Charts drawn from the data gave scientists a rough idea of the shape of mountains buried under the ice.

If the Seattle team could find out more about the electrical properties of the ice, the information would benefit other branches of science as well as their own.

"Our area of research," Irene explained, "was an interface between geophysics and upper atmosphere science—by way of electrical engineering. The work I went there to do was part of an overall study that had been going on for several years at Seattle and Stanford. We were studying properties of the lower ionosphere over the polar regions."

The ionosphere, one part of earth's atmosphere, is made up of thin layers of oxygen and nitrogen atoms that have been ionized—electrically charged—by high-frequency radiation particles, mostly from the sun. Some electromagnetic waves can travel from the earth to outer space, passing through the ionosphere with no trouble at all. But long, low-frequency radio waves are stopped abruptly, the way visible light is stopped by a brick wall, and simply bounce back to earth. Irene Peden and her group were making use of this mirror property of the ionosphere.

"We were going to send some very low frequency signals along a path which was over the ice but under the ionosphere," she explained. "Signals would be bouncing back and forth along the way. We knew what the signals were like when they were sent and when they were received at the other end, but we wanted to study the changes that took place in between. This information would tell us something about the properties of the reflecting boundary layer at the top. We hoped it would also tell us something about the material content of the ice at the bottom—more than a mile beneath the surface."

"People had studied the dielectric properties of distilled water in the lab," Irene explained, "but that doesn't apply very well to natural ice masses with varying impurities and varying temperatures, depths, and crystal structures."

The problem was a mathematical one that might be solved by a computer—but first the computer needed instructions and numbers to work with. Irene and her team worked out a mathematical model. The model described the properties of an electric or magnetic field radiated by the 21-mile Longwire antenna, along a base line perpendicular to and bisecting it. The base line stretched from Longwire station to "Downtown Byrd," fifteen miles away.

Before leaving Seattle, the scientists had programmed the computer to plot a set of curves, using their mathematical model and a lot of different combinations of numbers they thought might possibly be about right. Later, after they had done actual measurements on the ice, they could put *measured* numbers into the computer and correct their previous estimates.

Once the early experiments had been launched in Seattle, Irene found herself in a quandary. As a scientist sponsored by the National Science Foundation, she was required to work on the ice. As a woman, she was barred by the U.S. Navy.

"The NSF had a policy," she explained, "that all principal investigators in Antarctic research should do some of their work there, to become familiar with the environment. Their belief was that you couldn't design effective experiments unless you had lived in that environment. You just have to be there to know what it's like—what is possible to do and what isn't— the kind of constraints you have to work under. Of course I wanted to go down there and do the work myself. But the Navy's position was simple and clear. I couldn't go."

Irene's sponsor at NSF was still hopeful. "Someday," he told her, "there are going to be women working on the ice. When that happens, we'll get you in."

And they did. During the 1969–70 summer season, the barriers against women researchers working on the Antarctic mainland fell, and the NSF asked the Navy to provide transportation for Irene Peden. The final answer was slow in coming.

September arrived in 1970 and Irene's plans were still up in the air. The experiment was outlined, equipment was ordered, schedules were set—but no word arrived from the Navy.

"NSF answered all the Navy's historical arguments about the absence of 'facilities for women.' Then they invited me to give a lecture at the annual orientation session for Antarctic scientists. I think they hoped the Admiral would come and realize I really was qualified to do the proposed research. Finally, I guess the Navy ran out of arguments. They said I could go—on one condition. I had to have a female traveling companion."

Time was running out. The Seattle team was ready to leave for New Zealand, but no qualified woman had been found to accompany Irene.

As zero hour approached, the NSF representative in Christchurch had an inspired idea. He telephoned the New Zealand Alpine Club and asked if any woman member would like to go to Antarctica. It had to be someone who could pass the physical—fast. There was no time for a leisurely search.

Julia Vickers volunteered. Luckily, she turned out to be the perfect candidate. The 27-year-old librarian at the University of Canterbury was an enthusiastic mountain climber, in superb physical condition. Her husband, Ray, had spent a year at Scott Base with New Zealand's Antarctic program. His accounts of that year were enough to arouse her keen interest.

When Irene's plane landed in Christchurch, she still didn't know whether the necessary companion had been found. "I thought I might be left on the tarmac when the plane took off for McMurdo. But Julia was there, ready to go! It was great having her. I had resented the condition imposed by the Navy, but I was thankful for Julia. It was good having a buddy to bunk with and talk things over with. During the next few weeks we became good friends."

A week after they met for the first time, the two women

Irene Peden and Al Chandler monitoring radio signals

were living under the ice at Longwire Station, eight hundred miles from McMurdo.

"It was like being in a submarine," Julia recalled, "long and narrow, everything extremely compact, with a constant throbbing of engines."

Irene described it as "like living in a house trailer with slightly wavy, bumpy floors."

The three trailer vans that made up the station were arranged in a U-shape, under a big Jamesway hut that covered them all. One van, at the base of the U, was their transmitter room. A second van held the kitchen, bathroom, and a photographic darkroom. The third was partitioned into an electronics laboratory and two tiny bunk rooms. The in-between space, sheltered by the Jamesway, served as a rather chilly living and dining space.

"There were six of us living in a space built for two," Irene remembered. "When Julia and I arrived on November 1, along with Al Chandler and John Shulz from my department in Seattle, we found two men already there. Tom Stanford, another University of Washington student, and a mechanic named Don had been there all winter."

Julia recalled that they managed very comfortably. "We soon settled into a routine," she said, "with everyone taking turns at doing the three main chores—cooking, washing dishes, and shoveling snow for water. You could have a shower as often as you liked—provided you shoveled enough snow."

"You had to shovel a heck of a lot of snow just to get a teacupful of water!" Irene added. "I remember the first time I tried to shovel enough snow to fill the boiler. Before it was even half full, I was running out of steam. I kept remembering one of the last things my husband had said to me, when he was carrying my suitcases out to the car in Seattle. He said— very firmly and sternly, which he doesn't ordinarily do—'Remember, Irene, that you are not a man. You don't have to do everything the men do. Just remember I said that.' As the shovel grew heavier and heavier, I remembered.

"Later, I had to tell the others that I just couldn't lift that shovel again right away. 'Maybe a week from now,' I said, 'but not tomorrow. I'll do something else—more cooking—wash all the dishes—anything. But I think if I had to shovel snow again tomorrow, they'd have to take me out of here prematurely—with the experiment undone.' "

Together, all the inhabitants of Longwire revised the duty list. The men insisted that they would do all the shoveling if Irene and Julia would accept double duty for cooking and dishwashing. Agreed.

The tiny station had conveniences unheard of in other parts of Antarctica. The bathroom had a shower, a flush toilet, and a washer-dryer for clothes.

"Just think of all the snow that had to be shoveled for that!" Irene marveled. "And the shower, too. Our station was a showplace of the Antarctic. Visitors came from all over the continent to see our shower. The boys promised to keep it functioning like the ones at home, but we soon discovered that it wasn't a good idea to take a shower every day—for more reasons than one.

"The climate is so dry that our skin cracked—always seemed rough and scratchy. And the cold didn't help. Our summer temperatures often dropped to minus thirty. That's not so bad, compared to winter days that drop to minus ninety, but with the wind blowing hard—as it always does—it seemed colder."

The women had been warned to take along plenty of creams and lotions and to keep their skin oiled all the time. They did, but the cold, dry winds seemed to blow away all the benefits of their conscientious treatments.

Dishpan hands were another constant problem—and not just from dishwashing. Irene had to learn to use metal tools in below-freezing temperatures without freezing her fingers. Like everybody else who works in the Antarctic, she wore heavy "bear-paw" mittens to protect her hands, but they were too clumsy to allow careful work on delicate equipment. When repairs had to be made outdoors, Irene learned to keep her tools warm inside her parka. If she had to use a screwdriver, she'd whip it out quickly, use it with a bare hand, then put it back under the warm jacket and replace her mitten.

There was a lot of dishwashing, too. "I never do dishes at home," Irene confessed, "but down there I did plenty of them—

usually when somebody else had cooked, without any particular thought about how many dishes would have to be washed. Hand creams and rubber gloves were a necessity."

After a few days at Longwire, Irene had little time to think about such minor irritations as dry skin. There were other problems. The experiment was being delayed because of missing equipment—particularly an electronic device they needed for synthesizing wave patterns.

Irene knew that the station was about to be closed, permanently, on December 1. November was already a week old. Less than a month to complete the experiment! How could they do it without the essential equipment?

"Every day, when we talked to McMurdo by radio, we kept asking if our equipment had arrived. They kept saying, 'We're doing our best to find it—but you'll have to hurry.' We were getting desperate. I was determined not to fail, after all the trouble NSF had gone through to get me there."

Without the missing equipment, failure was an uncomfortable possibility. But salvation arrived, just in time. A visitor from Byrd Station offered to lend them a frequency synthesizer used earlier by the Stanford University team. Maybe it could be adapted for Irene's purposes. It was buried, he said, in a 40-foot-deep hole, somewhere near Byrd. If Irene wanted to come and haul it out, she could have it. Did she want it?

"Did I want it!" Irene exclaimed. "I was ready to zip up my parka and go after it."

The weather looked threatening, but Irene and her assistant, Al Chandler, set out with the trackmaster. The distance wasn't great—only sixteen miles—but it took them all day to complete their mission.

"We probably shouldn't have started out, with the weather

so close to whiteout," Irene remembered, "but we felt we had
to go. We were running out of time. Really desperate. It took
three or four hours to cover the distance. Most of the way we
could hardly see where we were going through the blowing
snow, but the flags that marked the path were still visible and
we followed them closely. We made it."

They found the storage place and Al descended into the hole
with ropes to tie around the synthesizer. Irene stayed on the
surface and held the other ends of the ropes, to keep them
from snarling.

"It took a long time to haul it out," she recalled. "My fingers
were icy cold. It was a difficult and delicate operation and we
had to be very careful. If anything had happened to that synthesizer, we would have been in trouble."

At the end of an exhausting day, the two scientists returned
to Longwire with their prize. Adapting it to suit their experiment
took longer than they had anticipated. By the time it was ready,
just one week remained before the station was to close. They
had to work fast.

"We had to work around the clock, in twelve-hour shifts,"
Irene recalled. "During that final week, on top of everything
else we had to do, we had a lot of visitors who wanted to see
the station before it closed. Sometimes we had as many as eight
or nine overnight guests—sleeping on the floor in sleeping bags.
Some of them even slept on the roof, in the space between
the vans and the covering Jamesway hut. We couldn't entertain
them, of course, but we had to cook for them."

There was a memorable Thanksgiving dinner—with frozen
turkey, and plastic flowers on the table. Somehow, the station
scientific leader found time to bake a pumpkin pie—without a
recipe. And somehow the experiment was completed.

Irene Peden mounted a loop antenna on a wooden sled.

On the day before deadline, Irene was out on the ice with a transmitter and loop antenna mounted on a sled.

"This is how we gathered the data we needed," she explained. "We turned on the transmitter and sent signals—with properties we knew—and received them along the base line, via the sled-mounted antenna. We measured the amplitude of the signals

Inside the trackmaster, Irene receives signals relayed from the moving antenna mounted on the sled.

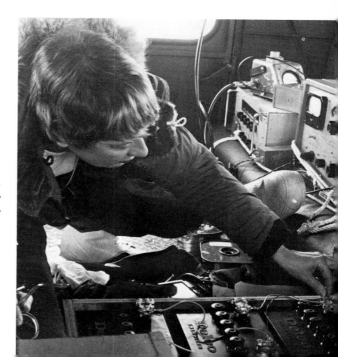

going away and measured the travel time. Later, in the computer program, we'd use those measurements to compare with our mathematical model—the one we had figured out in Seattle before we left. Nothing fancy, but it worked."

Triumphantly, the scientists gathered up their data and packed up to go home. Once more they piled into the trackmaster for a slow journey to Byrd, then were flown to McMurdo to wait for a flight to New Zealand.

Recalling Project Longwire ten years later, Professor Peden found the adventure still fresh in her mind.

"The work we did seems obsolete now," she said. "Ten years is a long time in radio science—but we laid the groundwork for more sophisticated research that came later."

Longwire Station is gone now—buried under the weight of accumulating snow and ice—but Irene's antenna was rescued. It was moved to another research station, Siple, where it is still being used by Antarctic scientists.

Six

A FRAGMENT
OF GONDWANALAND

Out in the Darwin Mountains, Rosemary Askin was climbing among the rocks, searching for tiny pieces of a jigsaw puzzle as big as the earth.

From time to time she stopped to measure a section of rock and enter a few figures in a small notebook. A sharp, cold wind, sweeping across the neighboring glacier, stung her cheeks and tugged at the notebook, almost snatching it from her gloved fingers.

Rosemary's eyes traveled over the rugged, gray landscape—so different from the green of her native New Zealand. The bare outcrop of rock on which she stood rose out of the surrounding ice like an island. Here there were no trees, no grass, no signs of life at all—except for a second human figure climbing and measuring another section of rock not far away.

When she looked down again, a layer of black rock caught her eye. A moment later, she spotted the fossil—the perfect print of a long, narrow leaf. With the trained eye of a paleontologist, Rosemary recognized the leaf and knew what it meant. This icy desert had not always been lifeless. There had been a

Rosemary Askin found clues in the rocks of Antarctica.

time, long ago, when the climate was warm and the land green. How long ago? Clues to that mystery lay buried in these rocks. Rosemary grasped her geology pick and began chipping out samples.

That was December, 1970, and Rosemary was in Antarctica as one of a party of eight geologists from Victoria University of Wellington, New Zealand. At twenty-one, she was the youngest scientist and the only woman on the team. By studying layers of rock, she and her companions were helping to write the history of an ancient continent. The group's leader, Peter Barrett, had already contributed a significant chapter. Now Rosemary was at work on another.

The New Zealanders were exploring a scientific mystery that had fascinated earth scientists for more than half a century. An early clue was a bag of rocks that had been discovered with the frozen bodies of Robert Falcon Scott and his men in 1912.

Those rocks contained clearly preserved prints of long, narrow leaves. The fossils had been found imbedded between seams of coal not far from the South Pole.

Paleontologists recognized the leaf prints as species of *Glossopteris,* a prehistoric plant that flourished in Africa and India some 200 to 300 million years ago. At the time, scientists were puzzled. How could they account for this evidence of a warmer, greener time at the bottom of the world?

Rosemary recognized the fossilized Glossopteris leaf.

Today, most earth scientists accept the idea that Antarctica was not always where it is now. They believe that Antarctica, Africa, South America, Australia, New Zealand, and India were once joined in a single continent—Gondwanaland. Some time in the remote past, the ancient land mass broke apart and the pieces drifted to their present locations on the globe.

Exactly when did Gondwanaland break apart? That was one of the questions that brought Rosemary Askin to Antarctica in 1970. She certainly didn't expect to answer the question all by herself. Other scientists, all over the world, were involved in the attempt to reconstruct the history of Gondwanaland. She intended to be one of them—to contribute a few clues.

Rosemary and her companions had concrete reasons for accepting the Gondwanaland theory, but acceptance was not universal. Even as late as 1970, some geologists resisted the whole idea of drifting continents. They rejected Gondwanaland as a myth—like flying saucers. The controversy had begun long before Rosemary was born.

When you look at any map of the world, you can see how neatly some of the pieces of land might fit together. South America and Africa, for example, might easily be two halves of a broken cookie. Other shorelines also seem to fit. The southern edge of Australia and the facing coast of Antarctica might have been drawn with the same stencil.

For as long as there have been reasonably accurate maps of the earth, observant people have noticed this remarkable matching of shapes. To account for it, scholars speculated about ancient catastrophes—earthquakes, floods, and sunken continents. "The Lost Atlantis" was a favorite explanation for a while.

Early in the twentieth century, a German astronomer and meteorologist, Alfred Wegener, developed a theory that all the land on earth was once a single mass. He called this supercontinent Pangaea. According to his theory, Pangaea had broken up gradually, over millions of years, and the pieces had drifted farther and farther apart.

Wegener's theory of "continental drift," first published in 1912, led eventually to the birth of a new science, plate tectonics. In recent years, pioneers in this field have discovered evidence that the earth's crust is made up of huge, rigid slabs that fit together in a giant jigsaw puzzle. The slabs, called tectonic (construction) plates, are rigid but not immovable. They float on the surface of a dense, molten underlayer.

During Wegener's lifetime he was ridiculed, but there were

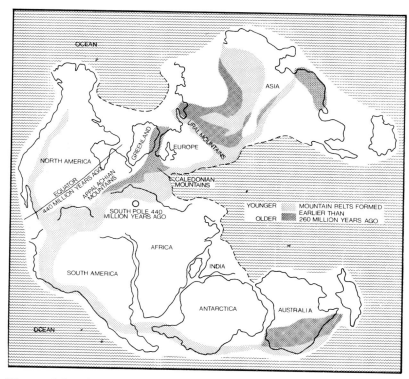

Wegener believed that all the earth's land masses were once joined in a single supercontinent, Pangaea.

a few scientists who did not scoff. In South Africa, Alexander DuToit, a respected authority on geology of the Southern Hemisphere, read Wegener's books and papers with interest. The two men exchanged letters for several years and supported each other's work. In their correspondence, they sometimes discussed Gondwanaland.

The name had been coined by an Austrian geologist, Eduard Seuss. In the 1890's, Seuss had suggested that India, Madagascar, and Africa might have been joined, long ago, in one ancient continent. He called it Gondwanaland, home of the Gonds, a prehistoric aboriginal tribe of India. His theory had nothing

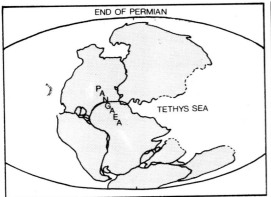 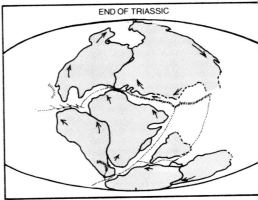

When the supercontinent broke up the pieces drifted—during hundreds of millions of years—to their present positions on the globe. Antarctic geologists found evidence

to do with the shapes of coastlines. Seuss was fascinated by the similarities between fossils discovered in the rocks of these separate lands. So was DuToit.

When Wegener died in 1930, his theory of continental drift was still obscure, but DuToit intended to change that. He embraced Wegener's theory and added it to the results of his own research. He had learned that many rocks and fossils of South Africa had identical twins in Australia, India, and South America. Plant fossils found in these widely separated places not only resembled each other but also matched the preserved leaf prints discovered by Scott's party in Antarctica.

DuToit was convinced that other Antarctic fossils, when they could be found, would provide the final proof that the continents had indeed been joined and that Gondwanaland was not a fantasy.

Antarctica, DuToit said, was "the key piece . . . around which, with wonderful correspondence in outline, the remaining puzzle pieces of Gondwanaland can with remarkable precision be fitted."

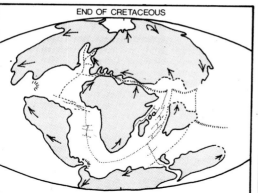
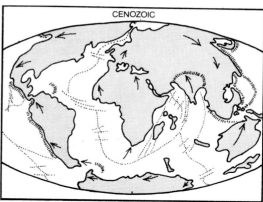

to support this "continental drift." Huge blocks of the earth's crust, floating on the surface of a dense, molten underlayer, fit together like a giant puzzle.

The South African geologist published his theory in 1937 and attracted a few supporters for continental drift. Just a few. The idea was so revolutionary that many scientists kept on resisting it until they were overwhelmed by evidence. As DuToit had predicted, the most convincing evidence was uncovered in Antarctica.

In the 1960's, as new techniques were developed for exploring and dating the earth's crust, more and more scientists supported the idea of continental drift. Still, the debate continued. Discoveries of fossil fish and plants, matching those unearthed on other continents, attracted a few more believers, but doubters demanded more proof. Where, they wanted to know, were the land animals? If Antarctica was once joined to other bodies of land, why hadn't explorers found animal fossils there?

The skeptics were given an answer when Peter Barrett discovered the fossilized jawbone of a primitive lizard in the rocks of Graphite Peak. Just after Christmas, on December 28, 1967, the young New Zealander and a field party from Ohio State University were working at an altitude of nine thousand feet, at the edge of the polar plateau. With his pick, Barrett turned over a piece of rock and saw something that looked like a fossilized bone.

Very carefully and patiently, Barrett and his field assistant, Dave Johnston, chipped out a channel around the bone. Some pieces broke off, but the two men wrapped them up and took them back to camp. There they glued the pieces together with pancake batter and speculated about what kind of bone it might be. It was obviously a jawbone—with strange-looking teeth.

When the field season ended, Barrett returned with the Ohio team to the United States and took his treasure to the Museum of Natural History in New York. Staff paleontologists identified the bone, definitely, as part of a Labyrinthodont, an amphibious lizard named for the complex, folded formation of its teeth. Remains of this primitive creature had been found in the rocks of Africa, Australia, and South America and were estimated to be about 220 million years old.

The New York Times, on March 13, 1968, ran a front-page story about the find. It declared: "The discovery supports the view that the [Antarctic] continent was once linked to other land masses."

Around the world, fossil scientists were excited and Gondwanaland theorists were ecstatic. Here was evidence—the first evidence ever found—that land animals with backbones once lived on the Antarctic continent. Suddenly, believers in continental drift were respectable.

Two-and-a-half years later, when Rosemary Askin was exploring the Darwin Mountains as Peter Barrett's field assistant, most geologists were convinced that Antarctica had once been part of Gondwanaland. The question that concerned them now was the problem of precise dates. When did Gondwanaland break

As the wind comes up at midnight, Rosemary Askin shovels snow onto the flaps of her tent at Escalade Peak, 1971–72.

apart? To answer this question, scientists like Rosemary looked for microscopic clues.

When she joined Barrett's team, Rosemary was a fourth-year student in paleobotany, the branch of geology concerned with fossil plants. Her specialty within that field was a comparatively new science, palynology, the study of fossil spores and pollen. These minute remnants of past ages were proving particularly useful for dating the rocks in which they were found.

Like grains of dust, pollen are too small to be recognized without a microscope. So, how can a palynologist know which rocks contain pollen fossils?

"You can't," Rosemary explained. "You just pick up the kind of rocks that *could* preserve pollen—and then you hope."

She knew which rocks to collect. Where leaf prints were visible, it was reasonable to suppose there were also pollen. More subtle clues appeared in the color and texture of the rocks.

For three months, Rosemary and her companions spent their days climbing among the rocks or sledding across snowfields and glaciers. Usually they worked in pairs, dividing the tasks involved in geological mapping, measuring layers of rock with a simple meter stick and level. When they found rocks needed for a particular study, they broke off samples to be analyzed later in laboratories at home.

They were nomads, moving their tents from time to time, whenever their work in a particular area was finished. In camp they shared the everyday jobs of cooking meals, gluing broken sled runners, melting ice every day for water.

"First thing every morning," Rosemary remembered, "we'd melt ice in a big billy-tin over our primus stove—then we'd make our morning tea and porridge. We brought along a powdered lemon drink to mix with the water we carried into the field every day, so we'd mix up a supply of that. Each of us filled a small plastic bottle with lemonade and carried it in a shirt pocket to drink during the day."

Working in the desert dryness, the geologists had been warned to drink plenty of water. Extreme cold, they knew, could paralyze the body's normal thirst mechanism and make them forget to drink. The little bottles of lemonade were a reminder, providing sugar for energy as well as necessary water. It was not a leisurely life.

"At night we were so tired, we didn't have time to be bored," Rosemary said. "We talked a lot, of course, but even after dinner we had plenty of work to do. During the days in the field we took notes in pencil in our pocket notebooks, then at night we'd go over the notes in ink. I always seemed to be days behind."

For their leisure time—scarce as it was—the scientists had

brought along a few diversions. Each member of the party carried a few books to read and exchange. Somebody had a chess set and a deck of cards.

"I think we were all surprised," Rosemary recalled, "at how little free time we had. Even during a whiteout, when we had to stay inside the tents for days at a time, I found I had plenty to do—just catching up with my notes and sleeping."

At the end of the season, Rosemary returned to Victoria University. When a shipment of rocks followed her to the geology laboratory, she was ready to begin the slow, meticulous process of getting the tiny pollen grains out of the rock and under a microscope. Each individual sample called for the repetition of a painstaking procedure.

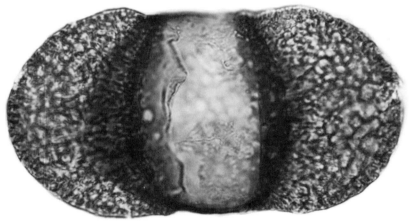

Magnified 11,000 times, this pollen grain was identified under the microscope by Rosemary Askin. From the Triassic period, it is about 200 million years old. She also found spores from the same period.

With a hammer—and then with mortar and pestle—Rosemary broke up small chunks of rock and dissolved the fragments in acid. The fossilized pollen grains, unaffected by the acid, were released from the rock. With endless patience, Rosemary concentrated the liberated grains, washed them, and stored them in alcohol. When she placed a few grains on a slide and examined them under a compound microscope, she could see the characteristic shape of each grain. These shapes helped her to identify the species of pollen and spores and to determine their approximate age—within a few million years.

Fossils of all kinds—animals, plants, or pollen—preserve a record of the earth's history. Rock formations containing fossils are like a library for geologists who know how to read them. Some specialists can read this history as clearly as other historians read old books and manuscripts.

For a history that goes back so far—perhaps four-and-a-half billion (4,500,000,000) years—geologists need a special timetable. Instead of days, months, and years, geologic time is measured in epochs, periods, and eras. To a geologist, an epoch of ten million years is hardly more than a few minutes of earth's history.

Through ages of geologic time, various forms of life were buried in successive layers of sand and mud that later hardened into beds of sedimentary rock. As types of plants and animals gradually changed through evolution, so different kinds of fossils are found in succeeding layers of rock. By studying the fossils, geologists can determine pretty accurately the sequence of rock formation. Higher forms of life indicate newer rocks.

Rosemary Askin's detective work involved "fine tuning"—a gradual narrowing of the estimated age of the rocks she examined. The fossil leaves she found in these rocks told her their approximate age. By comparing the pollen with similar pollen found in other parts of the world and already dated, she could determine more precisely how long ago they had fallen from living plants.

TIMETABLE OF EARTH'S HISTORY

ERA	PERIOD	EPOCH	YEARS AGO
CENOZOIC (Age of Mammals)	Quaternary	Recent	c. 10,000
		Pleistocene	1–2 million
	Tertiary	Pliocene	
		Miocene	
		Oligocene	
		Eocene	
		Paleocene	65 million
MESOZOIC (Age of Reptiles)	Cretaceous		
	Jurassic		
	Triassic		225 million
PALEOZOIC (Age of Invertebrates)	Permian		
	Late Carboniferous		
	Early Carboniferous		
	Devonian		
	Silurian		
	Ordovician		
	Cambrian		570 million
PRECAMBRIAN (the earliest years of Earth—almost 4 billion)			4,500 million

In the rocks she collected during the austral summer of 1970–71—her first season in Antarctica—Rosemary found the clues she had hoped to find. Her samples contained direct evidence for the age of glacial beds and overlying river-deposited sediments in the Darwin Mountains and southern Victoria Land.

"The broad age of the rocks had been determined earlier," she said. "We knew they were late Carboniferous to Triassic—somewhere about 200 to 300 million years old. I wanted finer dating. The pollen I had found were identical to species discovered in Australia. I had hoped this would be so, and the Antarctic fossils made it possible for me to compare them with fossils from Australian sequences and narrow the age."

Some of the rocks turned out to be younger than had been supposed. Rosemary labeled them "latest Triassic"—maybe no more than 190 million years old. Another piece of the Gondwanaland puzzle fell into place. Apparently, Antarctica and Australia were still joined as recently as 190 million years ago.

Fascinated by this Australian connection, Rosemary spent a part of the following year in Australia studying with Brisbane palynologist Noel de Jersey and paleobotanist John Rigby, who had also worked in the Antarctic. She was there again in August, 1973, when an international Gondwana symposium attracted geologists from around the world to Canberra, the Australian capital.

Gondwana specialists from as far away as Zambia, India, and the Soviet Union presented their evidence to the assembled scientists. Rosemary was there to contribute her findings. In collaboration with Peter Barrett, she delivered her first scientific paper. A few months later she was back on the ice, collecting more rocks for a Ph.D. dissertation.

During the next few years, Rosemary did a lot of traveling. She earned a doctorate and moved to the United States for postdoctoral work at the Institute of Polar Studies at the Ohio State University. Antarctic geology had become a habit she didn't want to change.

In early 1980, ten years after her first trip to Antarctica, she was ready to head south again, for the fourth time.

"It's a lot easier now," she said. "The first time I went, the U.S. Navy raised a few objections—because I was the only woman on the team. They could have refused to take me. But they didn't. Now it doesn't make much difference whether a scientist is a man or woman—it's the science that counts."

Seven

NATURE'S
ANTIFREEZE

In an improvised aquarium near McMurdo, Yuan Lin DeVries moved among the plastic swimming pools that served as tanks for a collection of huge Antarctic codfish. Slowly, rhythmically moving their fan-shaped fins, the dark-gray fish propelled themselves around and around in the cold running sea water piped in from McMurdo Sound.

Some of the fish weighed at least 150 pounds, half again as much as the young woman who watched them. Their big mouths opened and closed solemnly, in contrast with the cheerful cartoons of smiling fishes painted on the outside of the pools.

An hour earlier, Yuan had injected each fish with a radioactive substance. Now it was time to take blood samples. She rolled up the sleeves of her plaid flannel shirt.

In September, 1974, Yuan was beginning her third season of research in Antarctica. McMurdo had become as familiar to her as the neighborhood in Taiwan where she grew up, or the lab at Scripps Institution of Oceanography, La Jolla, California, where she worked as a biochemist. She felt as much at home in the aquarium on the ice as she had been on the Univer-

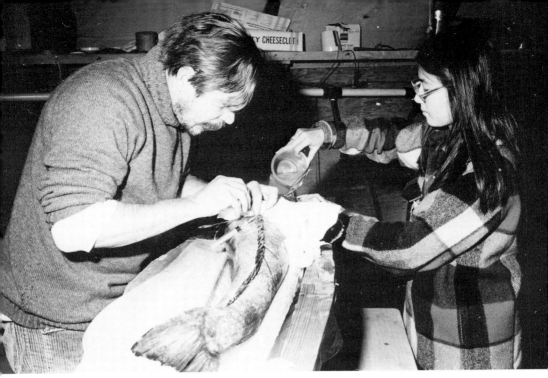

Yuan and Arthur DeVries take blood samples from a giant Antarctic codfish,
Dissostichus mawsoni.

sity of California campus at Davis, where she had studied for
a Ph.D.—and met Arthur DeVries.

It was DeVries who influenced Yuan to become a polar scientist. When they met in 1970, he was doing post-doctoral work
at Davis after receiving a Ph.D. from Stanford University. He
had spent several seasons in Antarctica with a Stanford research
team and already had made a major discovery—the kind of
achievement every scientist dreams about.

In the blood of the giant Antarctic cod, *Dissostichus mawsoni,*
Arthur DeVries found the answer to a question that had puzzled
biologists for years: What keeps Antarctic fish from freezing
to death in water that is colder than the freezing point of their
blood?

DeVries tackled the question with determination and came
up with a very definite chemical answer. The blood of these
fish contains a natural antifreeze—a protein molecule that was
unknown until Arthur DeVries isolated it. Proteins, the basic
building blocks of life, are made in almost infinite variety. This
one was a glycoprotein.

The more he learned about this natural antifreeze, the more
he wanted to know. How did the fish's body make the substance?
How did it work? Did other fishes have it? There were dozens
of questions to be answered.

When DeVries met Yuan Lin at Davis and told her about
his work, she seemed as fascinated by it as he was. She understood what he was trying to do. Soon after he went to Scripps
as a research physiologist, Yuan arrived there to work as a biochemist. Arthur continued his research with the Antarctic cod
and Yuan soon became part of it.

"I did a lot of the lab work on samples Art brought from
McMurdo," Yuan recalled. "Most of it involved biochemical

analysis—isolating proteins. Art went back to Antarctica every year, but it didn't really occur to me that I might go there, too. At that time, it was something you just didn't think about—not if you were a woman. It seemed impossible."

Yuan knew that a few women had been accepted by the United States Antarctic Research Program, but they were very rare. She had heard about Christine Muller-Schwarze who had accompanied her husband as co-researcher—and a few others. Still, she was surprised when Arthur DeVries told her he had spoken with his sponsor at the National Science Foundation about the possibility of including Yuan in his research team the following year. It was an inventive way of asking her to marry him.

When the news arrived from NSF, it was almost a wedding present. Yuan and Arthur DeVries were married in the summer of 1972. A few months later they were settling in at McMurdo and Arthur was showing his bride how to catch a fish through the ice.

"Art did the fishing," Yuan explained. "Sometimes I went along to watch, but it was a heavy job—too heavy for me. Some of the fish weighed as much as he did. The ice was so thick that the Navy had to drill a hole for us. Then Art set up a winch and line, dropped the line through the hole—with baited hooks—and left it there for twenty-four hours. The next day he'd go back to pull up the fish."

Yuan was the only woman living at McMurdo during that first season. One or two other women turned up from time to time, on their way to other parts of the continent, but Yuan's daily companions were her husband, fellow scientists, and the Navy staff—all men.

"I wasn't lonely," she recalled. "Art was there and we were

"We saw the same people every day. . . ."

together. Our living quarters were comfortable and the weather wasn't bad. The only drawback was the sameness. Sometimes that bothered me—a little. There was daylight all the time. And we saw the same people every day—worked with them, ate with them—if we went to a movie the same people were there. But Antarctica was new to me and the work was exciting.''

At the end of the austral summer, Yuan and Arthur returned to California with enough blood samples to keep them busy in the lab at Scripps. Yuan isolated more of the antifreeze substance and had some of it radioactively labeled for use in future experiments. Both researchers already had ambitious plans for the following year and could hardly wait to work out the details.

In September, they headed south again on "winfly"—the first plane to land at McMurdo at the end of winter isolation. Arthur was eager to start fishing as early as possible. Immediately after they arrived, he started to work with a Navy team—drilling holes through the six-foot-thick ice and placing heated shacks over the holes. Navy construction workers had already set up the new aquarium on the ice and had installed the plastic swimming pools with flow-through pipes for sea water.

Both husband and wife had plenty to do. During the first few weeks, Arthur spent most of his time out on the ice. He started a tagging program—catching the giant codfish, weighing them, attaching numbered tags, and releasing them. In later years, if he caught one of the tagged fish, he could find out how much it had grown. More fish had to be caught for laboratory studies. He and Yuan inserted plastic tubes into the veins of a few fish, making it easier to monitor their body fluids.

"We were trying to find out where in the fish's body the antifreeze glycoprotein was made," Yuan explained. "We also wanted to know more about the distribution of the substance within the fish—which body fluids contained it. Then we were investigating the rate of turnover of the antifreeze in the blood of the fish. For that we used the radioactive antifreeze compounds we had prepared in the lab at Scripps."

Yuan injected the radioactive substance into the veins of the fish. Later, at definite periods, she took blood samples to measure the concentration of radioactivity and to see how long it remained in the blood. At first she took samples every hour—then every day—then at longer and longer intervals.

Years later, Yuan recalled her second season at McMurdo as her favorite in Antarctica—partly because they were there for the arrival of spring.

"There were still a few hours of darkness when we first arrived," she said. "The sun was never quite all the way up. Then the days grew longer and the sky changed color. It was beautiful—a sort of peachy-cream color all around you. I'll never forget it!"

Later in the season two more women joined Yuan in the biology laboratory at McMurdo. Mary Alice McWhinnie and Sister Odile Cahoon were about to become the first women scientists to remain there all winter. When Yuan and Arthur left for California, Dr. McWhinnie was ready to take over the duties of chief scientist at the station.

"There were a lot of changes at McMurdo," Yuan recalled, "between my first season—when I was the only woman—and my third and last, 1974–75. More women turned up during that season, including Navy women and several civilian secretaries for NSF."

Yuan DeVries took this dramatic picture of a skua.

When the DeVrieses arrived at McMurdo in September, 1974, again on the earliest flight, they brought with them a dozen black codfish from New Zealand. In the aquarium, they made room for these fish in one of the plastic pools and proceeded to introduce the newcomers to some of the rigors endured by their Antarctic cousin, *Dissostichus mawsoni.* Could the New Zealand fish survive at subzero temperatures? Would they begin to synthesize their own antifreeze glycoprotein as the larger fish had done?

No, they couldn't. A few of the new fish were tested in a tank where the temperature was lowered to match the cold water of McMurdo Sound. The fish died. So—the remarkable antifreeze glycoprotein was not easily made by just any fish.

In another experiment, Yuan and Arthur gave transfusions to a few of the New Zealand cod, using glycoproteins isolated from the blood of the Antarctic fish. When the temperature in their tank was lowered to almost two degrees below freezing, the transfused fish survived.

Every experiment revealed something new—some kernel of knowledge that triggered new questions and more experiments. The California researchers caught and tested other species of Antarctic fish, to see what kind of antifreeze kept their blood from freezing. They found glycoproteins similar to those isolated from the codfish. One exception was a fish hauled up from the deepest part of McMurdo Sound, where the water wasn't quite so cold. This fish, unknown before Arthur DeVries discovered it, was later named for him—*Paraliparis devriesi.* It froze to death in colder water, where the cod survived.

As their discoveries and questions multiplied, Arthur and Yuan found themselves reaching beyond the Antarctic. What about northern fish? Some of them, like the winter flounder found in waters off the eastern coast of Canada and the northeastern United States, also swim under the ice in winter. How do they do it?

"We were interested in northern fish, too," Yuan said. "We sort of assumed that they must have something in their blood to keep them from freezing in cold weather, but nobody had ever isolated it. We wanted to find out what it was. But first we'd have to catch large quantities of fish in order to get enough blood samples to study. The winter flounder is much smaller than the Antarctic cod. From each fish you may get two or three milliliters of blood, so you'd need several hundred fish to get enough to isolate anything significant."

Between seasons at the bottom of the world, the young scientists sometimes turned their attention to the top half, but it wasn't an easy matter to collect the fish they needed. The project called for detailed planning and expensive equipment.

"You can't just get off a plane in Nova Scotia and go to the beach and catch five hundred fish right away," Yuan said. "In the Antarctic, everything was all set up for catching fish—mainly because Art worked there for so many years and gradually built up the facilities. But in the Northern Hemisphere we didn't have a base to work from."

The opportunity to find out more about northern fish came one summer when a student of Arthur's, Jack Duman, was working at a university in Nova Scotia. He caught hundreds of winter flounder, collected their blood, and shipped it to the DeVries laboratory at Scripps.

The blood of the winter flounder was full of surprises. The biochemical analyses revealed an antifreeze ingredient—as Yuan expected—but it was not a glycoprotein like the antifreeze isolated from the Antarctic cod. This was a very different com-

pound—a peptide chain made up of several amino acids. Yuan
was fascinated.

"Eventually we found more differences between the antifreeze substances in northern and southern fish," she recalled.
"The Antarctic cod have antifreeze in their blood year round.
They need it in McMurdo Sound where the temperature of
the water stays almost constant—about minus two degrees Centigrade. But the winter flounder make antifreeze only in winter.
They don't need it in summer when the North Atlantic warms
up."

By 1976 the study of winter flounder had become Yuan's
special project. The DeVrieses moved from Scripps in California
to Urbana, Illinois, where they set up a new laboratory at the
University of Illinois. After that, Arthur continued the Antarctic
research, returning to McMurdo every year, while Yuan focused
most of her attention on the winter flounder. She received a

An improvised aquarium for experimental fish at McMurdo Station

separate grant from NSF to pursue this biochemical mystery.

"What interests me most is the on-and-off control of the anti-freeze in winter flounder," she explained. "What tells the fish, 'Now you'd better start making antifreeze'? Then, in summer, some signal comes along and tells them, 'You don't need it any more.' What is the signal? That's what I'm looking for. I'm far away from an answer, but that's what I'm after."

While Yuan explored the chemical secrets of winter flounder, Arthur investigated parallel questions about Antarctic fish. Why do they have no stop-and-start mechanism for making antifreeze? Did they ever have such a control? Or did they evolve without it?

Year after year, at both ends of the globe, Yuan and Arthur DeVries found more answers to their questions—and each answer generated a new list of questions. Yuan didn't go back to Antarctica after 1975, but Arthur returned to McMurdo every year. While continuing his own work, he still found time to introduce other scientists to the special techniques of fishing through six feet of ice.

Meanwhile, the glycoprotein antifreeze discovered by Arthur DeVries became a useful research tool for other specialists. One of these, Professor Audrey Haschemeyer, a molecular biologist from Hunter College in New York, organized her own Antarctic project.

Eight

FUNDAMENTAL QUESTIONS

After an early breakfast of bacon and eggs at the McMurdo mess hall, Audrey Haschemeyer jogged down to the aquarium on the ice. All the plastic pools had been freshly stocked with fish and she was impatient to make a start on a new set of experiments.

For Professor Haschemeyer and her colleagues from Hunter College, Antarctic fish were providing answers to some fundamental questions about human biology. Scientists can learn a great deal about the complex chemistry of the human body by studying simple animals. In fish, Audrey Haschemeyer was exploring questions that once seemed unanswerable:

How long does it take a living cell to manufacture a single protein molecule? How do changes in temperature affect this process? What is the role of certain hormones in human metabolism? Exactly how do these hormones work?

Questions like these have always fascinated Audrey. She tackled some of them even before she received her Ph.D. from the University of California at Berkeley in 1961. The quest for answers led her, seventeen years later, to Antarctica. There

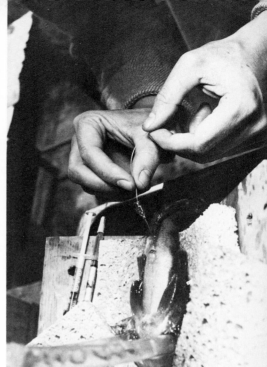

LEFT: *Audrey Haschemeyer photographed in the lab at McMurdo.* RIGHT: *Audrey inserting tubes into the veins of fish.*

she intended to learn from polar fish how temperature changes can affect some of the complex life processes in humans.

"Fish are very much like us—from a biochemical point of view," Dr. Haschemeyer said. "They are vertebrates—have backbones as we do. The proteins in their bodies are similar to ours, and they do some of the same jobs."

Early in the 1970s, Professor Haschemeyer and a team of molecular biologists at Hunter College in New York City were studying the effect of temperature changes on several life processes. Their special interest was metabolism—the constant buildup and breakdown of proteins inside every living cell.

"We're trying to make measurements—inside living fish— to tell us how fast some biochemical reactions go," Audrey explained. "An unusual aspect of our method is that we work with *live* fish. Most biochemists work in test tubes. We do, too—some of the time—but we also measure reactions in the living animal."

The Hunter biologists actually timed, with a stopwatch, the making of specific protein molecules as they watched the movement of nutrients between blood and tissues.

"Our experiments are very complicated," Audrey explained. "We insert tubes into the living fish and run in materials that we follow as they move through the tissues of the fish. Afterward, we run a detailed biochemical analysis that requires some very sophisticated equipment."

One summer, while working at the Marine Biological Laboratory at Woods Hole, Massachusetts, Audrey and her team made a series of precise measurements involving a toadfish. It took about five minutes, they discovered, for the fish to make a protein molecule when the water was a normal 20 degrees Centigrade. As they gradually cooled the water, the process took longer and longer. By the time the water reached three degrees, just above freezing, it took six hours. The manufacturing process was still going on, but very, very slowly.

"When these fish get down to about ten degrees Centigrade, they begin to shut everything off," Audrey said. "They look dead, but they don't die—just go into a sort of hibernation state. For us, that was inconvenient. It meant we couldn't study some processes at these low temperatures—because the systems didn't function. Sometimes there was no activity to measure."

Audrey knew that Antarctic fish were another matter. In icy McMurdo Sound, fish swam around normally and seemed unaffected by the cold. With growing interest, she read reports about the antifreeze protein isolated from McMurdo fish by Arthur and Yuan DeVries. One of her graduate students, Alan Hudson, went to McMurdo in 1975 to see if he could find out how the fish made this remarkable protein.

In the Antarctic codfish, Hudson was able to repeat some of the experiments he had done with Dr. Haschemeyer in temperate-zone fish. At low, low temperatures that would have sent a Woods Hole fish into a cold coma, the Antarctic fish manufactured a protein molecule in just twenty minutes. There were a lot of things this fish could do that the toadfish couldn't.

"Alan brought back the data," Audrey recalled, "and we published a joint paper with DeVries about those experiments. Alan raved about Antarctica—how wonderful it was—and I began to think we should develop this research further. The work we were doing at Hunter could be marvelously extended if we could study fish at those extremely low temperatures. Nobody else had looked at the molecular basis for the adaptation process in Antarctic fish—so we would be doing something new."

While the collaborators were at work on their joint publication, Audrey found herself thinking more and more about Antarctica. In the spring of 1977, she submitted to the National Science Foundation a proposal for a three-year research program at McMurdo.

While waiting for a reply, Audrey was deeply involved in another project in a very different part of the world. As chief scientist aboard the *Alpha Helix,* a research ship operated by the Scripps Institution of Oceanography, she went off to the Galapagos Islands to study tropical fish.

The name of the ship had special significance for Audrey. This molecular biologist, whose textbook on proteins is used in university classrooms, is very familiar with "alpha helix"— the spiral structure of a peptide chain found in many proteins.

Arthur DeVries (left) introduces the Hunter College team to the aquarium. Project Leader Audrey Haschemeyer (next to DeVries) was assisted by Rita Mathews, Wayne Van Voorhies, Michael A. K. Smith, and Alan Hudson (behind Audrey).

When she returned from the Galapagos, Audrey received word from NSF that her Antarctic proposal had been approved. A year later she was on her way to colder waters. In October, 1978, she saw Antarctica for the first time.

"I had seen the orientation films," Audrey recalled. "I'd heard descriptions from Alan and DeVries and others who had worked at McMurdo and I thought I knew exactly what to expect. But I was unprepared for the impact of the scenery—the way the light changes from hour to hour—all the different colors. Antarctica isn't a white continent at all."

As principal investigator for the new project, Audrey had

chosen her team carefully: Dr. Rita Mathews, who had earned a Ph.D. in the Haschemeyer laboratory at Hunter; Michael Smith, an exchange student from England; and Alan Hudson, who had been to McMurdo before. Arthur DeVries introduced the newcomers to the laboratory and aquarium and offered to help them catch the fish they needed for experiments.

"We were fishing all the time, constantly restocking the tanks," Audrey said. "It's not easy to collect fish through the ice, but we had expert help."

On a typical fishing expedition, the scientists went out by helicopter to look for cracks in the ice. In spring and summer it wasn't always necessary to drill holes through several feet of ice—not if they could find natural openings.

"DeVries usually knew where to look," Audrey said. "When

LEFT: Dr. Rita Mathews worked with Audrey Haschemeyer at McMurdo. RIGHT: The complex experiments called for some very sophisticated laboratory work.

we found a good place, we'd land, set up our traps, and leave them overnight. Next morning, somebody would fly out to collect the catch.''

Occasionally they camped on the ice, but their home at McMurdo was the Mammoth Mountain Inn. Its grandiose name had been given with good-humored irony. Like other buildings in the sprawling research station, the Inn was a plain, serviceable structure. Audrey and Rita shared a room.

"We had two narrow bunks, a table, and two narrow lockers for our clothes," Audrey recalled. "That was all that could be squeezed into our room—and it was cramped."

"The walls were not exactly soundproof," Rita added. "We could hear every snore in the building. But we adapted. Besides, we spent most of our time in the lab."

The Ecklund Biological Center was another story. Both women agreed that it was efficiently equipped for the kind of work they were doing. There were a few very specialized tools— like the high-speed centrifuge, for separating the components of fish blood, and a scintillation counter for measuring radioactivity in some of the tracer chemicals they used.

Audrey knew exactly what she was looking for. The remarkable antifreeze protein found in Antarctic fish offered several exciting challenges to a molecular biologist. She knew what the protein was made of—how each molecule was assembled, piece by piece, from amino acids, strung like beads on a chain according to a predetermined blueprint. But where did the blueprint come from? Did the Antarctic fish inherit this gene from some remote ancestor?

"We wanted to trace the whole heredity sequence for the protein," she said. "It is a very unusual protein. There is nothing else like it, that we know of, in the biological kingdom. It uses only two amino acids—of the twenty available for making proteins—and uses them in a repeating sequence that never varies. This repeating sequence tells us that there must be a gene that is also repeated. Such a gene would have some very interesting properties. We want to find out what they are."

Another unusual thing about the antifreeze protein is that there is so much of it in the blood of Antarctic fish. About half of all the protein in their blood is this special protein. No other fish has so much of one kind of protein. Fortunately for the Hunter biologists, there was plenty of it available for their experiments at McMurdo. They had ambitious plans.

"We could set any schedule we wanted," Audrey recalled. "With twenty-four hours of daylight, we weren't limited—but we finally arrived at a schedule that allowed for regular meals and enough sleep and recreation. The galley was open for breakfast from six to seven-thirty every morning, but we soon discovered that everything would be gone if we waited too long. We needed a good breakfast for the demanding work we were doing, so we usually managed to race over to the galley by seven every morning—then we'd be in the lab before eight."

The researchers worked until lunchtime. Then, after a break, they'd go back to the lab until five or five-thirty. The next hour was free for whatever they wanted to do. Audrey practiced her singing and sometimes jogged over to Hut Point, where the little wooden house built for Scott's 1902 expedition still stands. She was always back again before six-thirty, closing time for the galley.

"The food was excellent," Audrey remembered. "Those Navy cooks are really good. Most people gain weight at McMurdo. You work off a lot of calories, but when you see three or four home-baked desserts at lunch and dinner, it's hard to resist *all* the time. At home, I don't tempt myself like that. I gained five pounds at McMurdo."

The extra pounds didn't keep her from winning first place among women running in the first annual Scott's Hut Race—five miles in 48 minutes and 43 seconds.

When she's at home in New York, Audrey jogs daily around the Central Park reservoir, not far from her Park Avenue apartment. In the Antarctic, in spite of cold and icy surfaces, she still felt the urge to run. At the end of a long day in the laboratory, she found it relaxing to jog out to Hut Point. On the road she often met other runners—and so the idea that grew into the first annual Scott's Hut Race was born.

"It was a real community event," Audrey said. "Everybody helped. The Navy public works people graded the roads—a tough job, considering the permafrost. AFAN McMurdo, the world's most southerly radio station, made a lot of announcements and encouraged registrations."

On the day of the race, December 3, 1978, so many people turned out to watch it that the AFAN announcer reported, "Half the base is on hand . . . so who's listening to us?"

A few New Zealand runners came over from Scott Base, two miles away, to participate. When the countdown began, eighty-nine runners had gathered at the starting line. Their five-mile course began at the biology laboratory, extended to the tip of Hut Point, turned up a steep hill to the cosmic ray laboratory, and back to the biology lab. In spite of the rugged conditions, only four people dropped out before the finish.

After the race the runners gathered in the McMurdo mess hall for a victory celebration and feast. The main course of the dinner looked familiar to the Hunter biologists. It was smoked Antarctic cod—*Dissostichus mawsoni.*

Nine

THE VOICE
OF THE SEAL

Under a vivid blue sky of mid-October, Jeanette Thomas steps outside the door of her wooden fish house and walks across the ice toward the Weddell seal colony. From a distance, the huge animals resemble black garden slugs, sunning themselves on the rocks like tourists on a Florida beach.

Right now the colony is a small nursery—mostly females with new pups and other females ready to give birth at any moment. As Jeanette approaches the outskirts of the colony, she starts to count, almost unconsciously—but her attention is focused beyond the seals on the rocks. At this moment she is listening intently to a strange, dissonant music.

The sound comes from below, penetrating the ice under her feet. Jeanette recognizes this underwater symphony. The seals are down there, diving and calling to each other under the ice.

"It's an eerie sound—a bizarre sound," she said later. "Everybody notices it as soon as they come near a seal colony in Antarctica. Some people say it sounds like a jungle. There's a feeling of constant calling all around you—all sorts of calls. When you

A microphone lowered through a hole in the ice by Jeanette Thomas picks up the calls of the seals swimming below.

read the journals of the early explorers, you see that they noticed it, too."

James Weddell, the nineteenth-century British sealer and explorer, reported that one of his sailors—on a voyage to the Antarctic in 1822—described a beautiful mermaid who swam along beside the ship "singing lyrically for two full minutes." When Weddell investigated the "mermaid," he found a seal— and gave it his name.

Apsley Cherry-Garrard, traveling with Scott in 1910, commented on the "grunts, gurgles, pipes, trills and whistles" made by the seals underwater. Later visitors compared the sound to "far-out electronic music" and "birds chirping in a room full of echoes."

When Jeanette Thomas first heard these sounds in 1976, she became so fascinated that she decided to record and analyze them for a Ph.D. project. Within a short time she was able to recognize many of the calls. Just by listening, she could tell when the seals were looking for food underwater, or when a male seal was staking out his territory during the mating season.

Within four years her work had attracted the attention of seal experts in far places. In the summer of 1980, at the invitation of the Soviet government, she spent three weeks in Siberia studying the vocal behavior of seals at Lake Baikal. But Antarctica remained her chief laboratory.

Before her first meeting with the Weddell seals, Jeanette had heard a great deal about them from her husband, Douglas De-Master. Both were students at the University of Minnesota when they married in 1975. At that time Jeanette had just completed her master's degree research—a study of meadow mice—and he had spent a season in Antarctica studying seals. His enthusiasm for the animals was so contagious that Jeanette wanted to see them, too.

"I heard that there was a spot available for a field assistant with the Minnesota team going to the ice in 1976," she recalled. "They needed somebody to help with the tagging and counting. My first intention was to go for one year—just for the experience—but once I had been there, I couldn't wait to go back."

Jeanette and Douglas had agreed when they married that she would keep her own name.

"I feel that it's important for all women to retain their identities," she said. "Not just scientists. For us, it was particularly important to keep our professional work separate. We are two

A young Weddell seal emerges from the snow.

independent researchers. I am an animal behaviorist and Doug is a population ecologist—so we really do very different things. His work involves estimating the longevity of the seals, learning how they survive, how often they reproduce, at what age they reproduce. My studies of the seal's vocalizations are quite separate."

In their separate areas, Jeanette Thomas and Douglas DeMaster were contributing to an overall study of Weddell seals begun in 1969 by University of Minnesota Professor Donald B. Siniff. From the beginning, Dr. Siniff had made use of television cameras and underwater recording devices in his research and always included an electronics engineer as a team member. During Jeanette's first season, when she heard the voices of the seals and saw the recording equipment, she recognized a chance to do research that had never been done before.

"Weddell seals are very vocal," she said. "They have a large repertoire. We've identified about 35 different calls that they make underwater and at least ten more when they're out on the ice. We're trying to find out what the various calls mean— then we can use them as biological indicators in our research."

Does this mean that Jeanette will be able to talk with the seals and understand what they are saying? When people ask her about this, she explains:

"It's not so much a matter of communication as identification. Once we know what the calls mean, our work will become easier. Right now we're asking ourselves what we can learn about mammals from their sounds. It's a nice technique. If you can learn by listening, you don't have to actually see the animal to know what it is doing. You don't have to tag it or capture it or bother it at all. You don't interfere with its normal activities. You can find out something about the animal without handling it."

To record the seal calls, Jeanette and her colleagues lower microphones into the water through holes made in the ice by the seals themselves. Like all mammals, seals breathe oxygen to stay alive, so they keep their breathing holes open by using their teeth—gnawing away the ice as it forms. Their calls, picked

Electronic monitoring devices help Jeanette Thomas analyze the voice of the seal.

up by underwater microphones, are recorded by monitoring devices on the surface. The scientists use a variety of systems.

"We have an automated system that's particularly helpful because you don't have to stay on the ice all the time to collect data around the clock," Jeanette said. "Our engineer, Larry Keuchle, worked out a system that switches on for two-and-a-half minutes every hour and records the sounds on a tape cassette. Once a day we go back and collect the cassette and put in a new one."

The tapes have to be played back and analyzed, a detailed process that keeps Jeanette busy for months after she returns from the Antarctic. For the first four years, most of her work was done in the little wooden fish house on the ice, about twenty miles from McMurdo. She described it in 1979, just before going to the ice.

"We go back and forth a lot, from McMurdo to the seal colony," Jeanette explained. "Usually we drive out to Hutton Cliffs in a tracked vehicle and stay several days at a time. We need to be close to the seals to understand what they are doing. For example, when they're having pups, we want to know exactly what time each pup was born. Then we can tag it and give it a number. I do a lot of behavior observation, so it's important for me to be there around the clock, to see how the time of day affects their behavior."

Weddell seals start having pups about the fifteenth of October. The Minnesota team usually arrives at McMurdo on one of the season's early flights—about October 5. The scientists use a lot of electronic equipment—cameras, microphones, and monitors—that must be set up ahead of time. They move into the fish house, stock it with food, and make sure the equipment works.

The house is small—just one room—twenty feet by fourteen

feet. It is furnished with bunks, table and chairs, and plenty of shelves, all crowded with cameras, tape recorders, tools, and supplies.

"We usually bring our drinking water from McMurdo," Jeanette said, "then we melt snow for other uses—like dishwashing and bathing. When we want a real shower and shampoo we go back to McMurdo. We take turns shoveling snow and cooking—all the household chores. For heat, we have a large oil-burning stove. We have to bring drums of oil from McMurdo but it's worth the effort. It keeps the house very comfortable and warm."

One year, 1978, Jeanette worked at sea in Antarctic waters aboard the *Hero,* recording the calls of leopard and crabeater seals. She spent other seasons in and out of the fish house on the ice and she feels right at home there now.

Hothouse blossoms, the only flowers in Antarctica, were presented to Jeanette Thomas when she visited Vostok, the Soviet research station, in 1977. Later, in 1980, Jeanette was invited by the Soviets to study the seals at Lake Baikal, Siberia.

"It's very cozy inside," she said. "We have a real floor, too—a wooden floor—not like the portable fish houses that are set up over the seals' breathing holes. We have windows on two sides. You can look out the back window and see an active volcano, Mount Erebus, smoking away. From the other window we can see the seal colony."

Her best view of the colony is from a small observation tower on top of the hut—with windows all around. Every day Jeanette spends hours in the tower, watching the seals through binoculars.

"We don't invade their colony," she explained. "The house isn't right in the middle of the colony, but it's close enough so we can see what they're doing at any time of day. Usually we visit the colony once a day, to see how many new pups there are. We tag the new ones and weigh the older ones to find out how fast they are growing."

The researchers are in no danger from the seals, even though the adult animals may be nine or ten feet long and weigh as much as half a ton. Weddell seals are placid, slow-moving creatures on land. Without legs, they can only creep like snails. In the water they become graceful, speedy swimmers and powerful divers, but they never attack humans—unless the humans harass them.

"The nice thing about studying seals is that they're so approachable," Jeanette commented. "They don't seem at all afraid of us. If you walk up to a seal, it will probably roll over with its head up. This is not like a friendly dog rolling over. The head-up posture is aggressive—a threat—but they won't chase you. If they roll over on their backs they're frightened, but they don't do this very often—and they don't crawl away and hide in the water when we approach them."

Compared with most large animals, Weddell seals are exceptionally tame—but they don't just lie down and allow the scien-

tists to punch holes in their flippers. If researchers want to attach
something to a seal they have to keep the animal still. It isn't
easy to hold an animal that outweighs you by hundreds of
pounds, but Jeanette has done her share of capturing and tagging.

"We usually work in pairs," she said. "One person puts a
bag over the head of the seal while the other ties up the animal
long enough to attach a battery or a numbered tag or radio
transmitter. We do the operation quickly, then release the seal.
They probably don't like it, but they don't protest violently.
The weather is so cold that the blood flow is sort of cut off
from the flippers, so they don't seem to feel the tagging much.
It's about like piercing your ears for earrings. We attach a plastic
tag to a flipper with a pair of pliers."

The tagging is part of a continuing census begun in 1969
by Dr. Siniff. Each year the scientists use a different color for
the tags. That way, they can tell a seal's age at a glance. An
orange-tagged seal was born in 1973. Blue means 1976. Sometimes they see tagged seals return to the colony where they
were born to give birth to pups of their own.

"The information we get from this program is important,"
Jeanette said. "In order to know how many seals there are,
you have to know how long they live, how often they reproduce,
at what age they reproduce. Those are the three main categories
of information we need. If we can mark individual seals and
follow these individuals through a lifetime, we'll gradually find
answers to our questions. The colored tags help us keep track
of seals that return, year after year."

Whenever Jeanette sees a newborn pup she gives it a tag
and number, but she is especially careful not to disturb it too
soon. Some animal mothers will abandon their young if humans
interfere.

A numbered tag, attached to a seal's flipper, makes it possible for scientists Jeanette Thomas and Valerian Kuechle to keep track of individual animals.

Jane Colin (right) and Donald Siniff, leader of the University of Minnesota team, bag an adult male Weddell seal with the help of Tony Eastley.

"We don't know that seal mothers would do this," Jeanette said, "but we do know, from studying other mammals, that there is a special pair-bonding during the first few days of life and it shouldn't be disturbed."

The scientists try to handle the seals as little as possible. They have to be captured briefly from time to time—for tagging, weighing, and attaching electronic equipment—but otherwise they are left alone. Jeanette's vocalization studies have already made it possible to gather a great deal of information about the seals' behavior without handling them at all.

Bioacoustics, the use of electronic surveillance techniques for studying animals, has just begun to be explored, Jeanette believes. She predicts that it will become more and more important to zoologists of all kinds.

"Minnesota scientists have been attaching transmitters to seals for years," she said. "These transmitters can be used for a lot of different things. In the past, we used them to monitor local movements and activity patterns. That is, you attach a transmitter to a seal—then later you go out in a helicopter or tracked vehicle and search for the signal. When you find it, you know where the animal is."

Until the 1979–80 season, the Minnesota team used this system to help them keep track of seals during the austral summer, but they had no idea where the animals went when they left McMurdo. That year, Jeanette became involved in a pioneer project that used earth satellites to monitor the migration of Weddell seals.

"Satellite monitoring is something new in the field of ecology," Jeanette said. "It has already been quite successful in the Arctic for tracking the movements of polar bears. Now several Antarctic projects are using it, too. Our pilot project gave us a chance to study our seals while testing a new technique for other scientists. Weddell seals are a good test species because they're large enough to carry transmitters without being harmed."

A variety of man-made satellites now orbit the earth in predetermined paths. Each satellite has been programmed to pick up specific kinds of signals in a particular code. The seals carry transmitters that send out signals—a constant *beep*ing that goes on as long as the batteries last. These signals can be picked up by a receiver installed in a buoy, somewhere in the path of the satellite. When the satellite passes over, at regular intervals, it receives the coded signals being relayed from the buoy and eventually transmits the information to a central receiver on the ground. Later, the information is decoded, analyzed, and interpreted.

"Before the satellite program started," Jeanette said, "we knew a lot about the seal's life during the spring and summer months, but nothing about its migrations in fall and winter. We know how long it takes to wean a pup and how long the mating season lasts, but after that they leave the colony and we can't follow them. The satellites make it possible for us to monitor the seals all winter without physically being there. We don't have to accompany them to know where they are."

Jeanette's fourth season in Antarctica, 1979–80, was her last with the University of Minnesota team, but it was far from the end of her Antarctic research. By January, 1981, she was there again, this time aboard an icebreaker, tracking killer whales as well as her seals.

Under a new NSF grant, she expanded her studies as a staff scientist for Hubbs Sea World Research Institute in San Diego. The voice of the seal—and now the whale—was calling.

Ten

THE LONGEST, COLDEST NIGHT

The poker players were in no hurry. The long polar night had just begun and they would have another five months to demonstrate their skill and luck. Some of the men were uncomfortable about letting a woman join the game, but Donna Oliver was doing her job like everybody else at McMurdo. She was the only woman on the base for the winter. If she wanted to play poker, why not let her try?

"At first they lowered the stakes for me, out of politeness to a woman," Donna recalled, "but when I began to win, they stopped making allowances. Pretty soon, I was an equal partner in the game."

It was a victory for Donna, considering the opposition some of the men had expressed when they learned that she was to stay on the base for the whole winter of 1977. Other women had worked at McMurdo during that austral summer, as Donna had done, but all of them were gone long before the sun went down in April.

Donna's position was unusual. She was doing two jobs that winter. As a laboratory technician, she worked with her husband,

John and Donna Oliver at the South Pole in 1975

John Oliver, and a team of marine biologists from Scripps Institution of Oceanography at San Diego. As an independent researcher and doctoral candidate in psychology, she was studying the effects of prolonged isolation on the small winter-over population of McMurdo. For this project she administered standard psychological tests to a group of volunteers, tape-recorded interviews, and noted her own observations of their behavior during the winter.

For Donna, the poker games were a chance to observe the men informally, and a chance to try to make friends with a few who seemed to resent her presence. Most of the opposition came from military enlisted men and construction workers who were there to maintain buildings and equipment.

"They made remarks to let me know how they felt," Donna said. "It was nothing personal—just a conviction that women, in general, don't have enough strength—physical or emotional—to put up with the kind of hardships these men expected to face during a winter of isolation. But before the winter was over, they changed their minds. A lot of the men who were toughest—the least happy about my being there—became my friends."

Before Donna Oliver challenged the prejudices of people who still felt that women couldn't stand the rigors of winter in Antarctica, only four other women had ever had the chance to try. Thirty years earlier, when Edith Ronne and Jennie Darlington spent an uncomfortable year with their husbands on Stonington Island, at least one of them concluded that women don't belong in the Antarctic.

When the first women scientists arrived on the continent in 1969, it was understood that they were there just for the summer. Only two women, Mary Alice McWhinnie and Sister Mary Odile Cahoon, had ever spent a winter at McMurdo before Donna and John Oliver arrived, in December, 1976, to stay for a full year.

John Oliver had been to Antarctica twice before, to study sea-bottom creatures that live under the ice. He was one of the Scripps biologists, led by Dr. Paul K. Dayton, who became the first human divers to swim in McMurdo Sound. Wearing rubber diving suits, they entered the water like seals, through holes in the ice.

Donna had worked as a technician in marine biology laboratories in California to pay for her graduate study in psychology. She had just completed her master's thesis when her husband was asked to make a third trip to Antarctica—this time to spend the winter. The Scripps team was to study the year-round habits of some of McMurdo's sea creatures and they needed a lab technician. John asked Paul Dayton to consider Donna for the job.

"I had done the type of thing they wanted done," Donna said. "They really did need somebody who could do what I had been doing in other laboratories. So Paul Dayton wrote to NSF and described my qualifications and experience. NSF gave me the usual tests—and I passed. I was finally approved for the job, but I'm told there was some debate before the decision was made. I was in suspense for five or six months."

Meanwhile, Donna saw a unique opportunity to do research for a doctoral dissertation. How often does a psychologist find a ready-made test situation in such an exotic setting? She was going to be part of a small group of people isolated at the bottom of the world. How would these people adapt to the harsh environment, to the absence of sunlight and familiar comforts? How would they behave when there was no mail from home, no fresh food, no way to leave the small, confined community? How would their behavior affect their companions?

In preparation for the study, Donna read everything she could find about earlier psychological and psychiatric research in Antarctica. While reading, she discovered unanswered questions—the ones she wanted to explore. When the message came from

Through a hole in the solid ice of McMurdo Sound, divers from Scripps Institution of Oceanography explore a hidden marine world.

NSF that she had been accepted as a member of the winter-over team, she packed up her tape recorder, notebooks, and a selection of standard psychological questionnaires. She also included a special test, designed by a Navy psychiatrist especially for Antarctic people, modified by Donna to include her own questions.

When Donna arrived at McMurdo in December, she was impatient to begin her tests and interviews, but she had to find time for them after her other work was done. Officially, she was there to assist the Scripps divers—to analyze the specimens they brought up from the sea bottom, to photograph the scientists at work, to pour hot water into their gloves to keep their hands from freezing. In her spare time, she was free to distribute her questionnaires and to interview the men.

During the first three months—the Antarctic summer—Donna was not the only woman at McMurdo. There were several scientists, a few Navy women, and a handful of secretaries and technicians. Toward the end of February, when all the winter-over people were preparing for the official "closing" of the station (no more new people until spring), Donna watched the other women leave and began to wonder if she really would be allowed to stay for the winter.

"Until the last plane went out on the first of March, I was afraid I might be sent out," she confided. "Nobody said so, but I knew it could happen. So I kept a very low profile—hesitated to remind anybody that one woman planned to stay all winter."

When winter began, seventy-eight men and one woman remained at McMurdo—the total population for the next six months. Donna had already administered one series of personality tests to forty volunteer subjects. Later, she could compare

LEFT: Donna Oliver pours hot water into her husband's gloves before he plunges into the icy water. RIGHT: During the winter, Donna let her hair grow long.

this information with results of other tests—given at the beginning, middle, and end of winter—to measure changes in attitudes and behavior.

Her aim was to examine both positive and negative effects of the winter-over experience. She had read a lot about some of the negative effects, described by earlier researchers as "winter-over syndrome." Certain symptoms, they found, were almost universal among winter groups at various stations. These included "driftiness"—a lack of concentration and a feeling that "the mind has been anaesthetized"—along with periods of depression and hostility. Nearly all of the men suffered from insomnia, for a while, and exchanged suggestions for treating or curing the "Big Eye."

"Big Eye," the most common complaint, had been the subject of one of the earliest biomedical projects in Antarctica. As early

as 1967, Dr. Jay Shurley, a research psychiatrist and professor
of psychiatry at the University of Oklahoma School of Medicine,
began a detailed study of the sleep patterns and dreams of men
who spent the winter at the South Pole. His methods included
medical tests and electronic surveillance, as well as traditional
interviews and observations.

Donna was familiar with Dr. Shurley's work and was particularly intrigued by his reports of *positive* effects of wintering at
the Pole.

"The effect of winter," Dr. Shurley reported, ". . . the geographical remoteness, cramped quarters and limitation of company at the South Pole induced the already self-sufficient,
controlled and calm men to become even more so."

Here was a statement that appealed to Donna's own optimistic
nature. She couldn't wait to find out how the group at McMurdo
would measure up. Six times during the winter she administered
standard tests—questionnaires used by psychologists everywhere—plus her own special test. Between times, she recorded
in her notebook her own observations of everyday happenings,
conversations with the men, and talk during the poker sessions.
Later, when she analyzed her findings, a pattern emerged. There
were high points and low points in group morale.

"The first major change occurred near the winter closing of
the station," Donna reported. "When the last plane flew out,
morale was high. Everybody relaxed, became acquainted at a
congenial pace, and marveled at the abrupt change from the
hectic summer chaos."

Like year-round residents of a resort town, the McMurdo
colony felt relieved when the "summer people" were gone.
Now the town was theirs. They looked forward to the challenge
of winter. On Donna's questionnaires, almost all of the men

said they were glad they had volunteered for the winter-over assignment.

Another noticeable change came after Midwinter Day, June 21. There was a widespread drop in morale. Donna's tests showed that many of the men felt depressed, tired, dull, and absentminded. The early excitement had worn off and they felt bored—seeing the same people every day, eating the same food, doing the same jobs, never seeing the sun. Their feelings were obvious, even without questionnaires.

"The slump was very real and easy to observe," she wrote. " 'Big Eye' was more common . . . and 'driftiness' also became more frequent. . . . Although these problems were troublesome, they were seldom so serious as to interfere with survival and task performance."

During the midwinter slump, the only woman at McMurdo might easily have found herself playing "mother" to a group of bored, dissatisfied men. Donna deliberately avoided that role—determined to remain objective in her study.

"I didn't encourage the men to bring me their problems," she said. "I had two jobs to do, so I couldn't take too much time away from my own work. As the winter went on, I did sense certain changes in their behavior toward me. They were just a little more formal in their treatment. They didn't swear around me. I knew they had cleaned up their language—but that was about the only special treatment they gave me."

In August, Donna noticed another abrupt change in morale. The men seemed to wake up and shake off their lethargy. They bustled around, talking about the things they had to do before "winfly."

"Winfly," Donna explained, "is the winter flight—usually about the first of September—the first plane to come in since

March. It brings mail, fresh food, and new people. For several weeks before it arrives, the winter-over group prepares for the newcomers. The low point of the slump is passed."

Like the first robin or crocus in more temperate climates, winfly means that spring is coming to Antarctica. Soon the research stations will open for the summer and the population of McMurdo will expand from about eighty to more than eight hundred people.

"The station opening demands team work and motivation," Donna said. "Winfly causes a dramatic shift in morale. Suddenly the station is beseiged by 150 newcomers, all excited and proud of their new exploration. Then the winter-over group unifies. . . . They are the Old Antarctic Explorers. The winter is over, they survived, and they now own the town."

The winter-over crew felt possessive and just a little bit supe-

Donna Oliver makes friends with a sled dog from Scott Base.

rior to the new arrivals. Donna heard some of them telling tall tales to unsuspecting newcomers, adding more and more hair-raising details until the naive listener began to suspect he was being tested for gullibility. She also sensed a complex mixture of feelings. Men who had waited impatiently for the plane that would take them home suddenly became reluctant to leave McMurdo. Before the plane arrived, they began to hope it would be delayed.

"Perhaps they feel that they have a more challenging, meaningful task to complete in Antarctica," she wrote later. "For one year they struggled to do their part in making the station safe for all its human inhabitants. The winter crew eventually became a close family, and for everyone to pull through the long, dark night safely was a rewarding accomplishment."

When she began her study, Donna had heard rumors of "psychological damage" caused by the long winter isolation in Antarctica. Her findings contradicted these rumors.

"Almost every person interviewed in the 1977 winter group considered the winter-over experience one of the best experiences of his life," she wrote.

Donna examined her conclusions carefully. Was it possible that she had influenced the test results by her own enthusiasm?

"I know that observations can be colored by the observer's own attitude," she said. "I'm sort of an optimist, so maybe I see the bright side of a statement and another psychologist might see pathology in it. That's where the tests help—to check the researcher's conclusions."

Donna had mixed feelings about psychological tests. At first she had intended to administer them to her subjects as a secondary part of the research. She started out with more faith in her own observations.

"In psychology," she explained, "there are people who believe in tests and people who don't. When I began my research in Antarctica, I had more faith in the phenomenological approach—the idea that the words that come out of a person's mouth mean more than test results."

When Donna analyzed the statistical data from the tests, she was surprised to find that it confirmed her conclusions based on observations.

"These results opened my eyes to the fact that tests do have value. I still don't think they're infallible, but they serve a purpose," she said. "Now I'm convinced that a combination works best—tests plus observations."

For Donna, herself, the year-long experience was definitely positive. She had done satisfying work, had completed the research for her dissertation, and had made new friends. When it was time to pack up and return to the United States, she found herself surrounded by well-wishers, all congratulating her and exclaiming, "Well, Donna, you made it!"

"I made it," she laughed. "What did they expect? Was I supposed to look pale and nervous? I had spent the winter eating good Navy food and had gained a little weight. I enjoyed the work I did. It was the most challenging and satisfying winter I ever had."

Eleven

TOO COLD FOR
THE COMMON COLD?

The scene could be science fiction, somewhere on the moon or a far planet. An isolated outpost stands in the middle of a featureless desert. Approaching from the air a traveler sees nothing but ice and snow in all directions—except a shiny igloo glinting in the sun.

The igloo is bigger than it looks from the air. Up close, you can see that it is a huge aluminum geodesic dome, big enough to enclose three two-story buildings. The entrance, through a wide arch of corrugated steel, is flanked by poles displaying bright flags flapping in a brisk wind. A sign over the entrance tells you that you're not on the moon. Big red letters on a white background proclaim:

THE UNITED STATES WELCOMES YOU TO THE SOUTH POLE

Landing at the Pole has become almost routine for Dr. Nan Scott, a Ph.D. microbiologist from Oklahoma. Nearly every October since 1973, she has arrived on the first plane of the summer season. She is always greeted by a handful of winter-weary men—and, more recently, women—who haven't seen

Nan Scott in the laboratory at South Pole Station

an outsider for eight months. They pretend to dread the needles Nan has brought to extract blood samples from their arms, but the mood is festive. After months of isolation, most of them will be going home at last.

"We always go in on the first flight," Nan explained. "We want to take blood samples from all the winter-over people before they've had time to be exposed to new viruses and bacteria that others will bring in during the season. There are usually about twenty people who have spent the winter and are just ending a full year at the Pole. Our object is to see what effect this long period of isolation has had on their resistance to infection."

The Pole is a unique laboratory for this kind of research. Nowhere else in the world is anyone so completely cut off for such a long time. For eight months, from February to Octo-

Dr. Harold Muchmore and Nan Scott prepare laboratory cultures.

ber, there are no arrivals or departures. It is so cold during the winter that no planes can land. If they did, the fuel would freeze in the tanks and they couldn't take off again. The only communication with the outside world is by radio.

Since 1978, a few women have shared this winter isolation, but Nan Scott can remember when women were a curiosity at the Pole—in any season. She and Donna Muchmore, a former hospital nurse, were the first females ever to work there. In 1973, the two women were assisting Donna's husband, Dr. Harold Muchmore, a medical specialist and professor of pulmonary and infectious diseases at the University of Oklahoma College of Medicine.

That year Dr. Muchmore had just begun a detailed study of certain changes that take place in the blood of people who are isolated from the rest of the world for long periods. He was especially interested in their resistance to diseases and the way their immunity patterns changed.

For years, men who worked in Antarctica had noticed that they were seldom sick while they were there. If they cut a finger or broke a bone, it would take a long time to heal, but it didn't get infected. They didn't even catch cold. After a while they began to assume that germs couldn't live in such a cold climate.

Most of these men were remarkably healthy anyway—only the healthiest are chosen to work in the Antarctic—but as soon as they went home they seemed to catch every germ that was going around. Something happened to their resistance while they were away. They were no longer immune to infections they had been able to resist before.

"I certainly don't claim to be the first person to have noticed this phenomenon," Dr. Muchmore said. "As early as 1968 or '69, my old friend Dr. Jay Shurley told me about a surprising discovery made by a Navy doctor who was with him at the Pole. Dr. A. B. Blackburn did a series of blood counts on the men who wintered over and discovered that the white corpuscle count in their blood dropped from 5,000 per cubic centimeter to 2,500 per cubic centimeter in nine months. Ordinarily, this would mean some terrible illness—maybe leukemia—but these men weren't sick. They were perfectly healthy."

About the same time, in the late 1960s, Russian scientists at Vostok station and Japanese researchers at Syowa made similar studies and came up with similar results. When Muchmore heard about these puzzling medical findings, he was interested, but never thought of becoming involved in them—until he dreamed of mirrors.

Dr. Shurley, a psychiatrist concerned with sleep and dream

studies, likes to tell the story of his friend's sudden vision of mirrors.

"When I first told Harold Muchmore about Blackburn's test results, I thought he'd be interested because he specializes in infectious diseases," Shurley recalled. "But he said he was busy enough studying sick people. The men at the Pole weren't sick—they were extra healthy. So what could he do that would help anybody? Then one morning he called me up, all excited, and said, 'Mirrors! I can do it with mirrors!' "

Dr. Muchmore confirmed the story. "My wife says I jumped out of bed that morning talking about mirrors. Apparently it occurred to me, while I was asleep, that I could look at people when they came out of Antarctic isolation and compare their health image with what it was before they went in. By this mirror image, I might be able to determine the sequential changes that took place in their immunities. By using each person as his own control—by using the same laboratory techniques I had used for people convalescing from sickness—I could learn what happened to these people who were convalescing from health."

Convalescing from health. The more he thought about it the more the idea interested him. Gradually, the project took shape in his mind. He would study every aspect of immunity that he knew how to study. It would involve collecting a series of specimens from each person and a lot of detailed laboratory testing. He was going to need an expert technologist with a lot of patience—so he thought of Nan Scott.

Before the project began, Nan was in charge of microbiology in Dr. Muchmore's research laboratory at the Veterans Administration Medical Center in Oklahoma City. When he asked if she'd like to go to the South Pole, she didn't quite believe it.

"I was excited over the prospect," Nan said, "but I didn't really think it was possible—until it happened. By that time a few women had worked at McMurdo—but not many. Some of them had visited the Pole, but they hadn't done research there."

Nan's first aerial view of the Amundsen-Scott South Pole Station in 1973 was very different from the one seen by visitors today. There was no geodesic dome then. The small station that existed was all but invisible from the air.

When the plane landed on the flat polar plateau, Nan and the Muchmores walked about half a mile toward a low hill where something bright and shiny reflected the sun. When they came closer they could see a striped pole—it looked like a barber pole—with a mirrored ball on top. A sign in front of the pole identified the spot as the South Pole, "ELEVATION 9186 FT. . . . POPULATION 21."

"The first thing I remember about the old station is the entrance," Nan said. "It was a dark hole with crude stairs leading down. We used to call them the holy stairs. You could go in that way or down a ramp that led into the garage, where tractors went in and out."

The little station had been built on the surface in 1956–57 for the International Geophysical Year, but sixteen years of blowing snow had buried it. By the time Nan arrived, it was twenty feet under the ice.

"Not quite buried," Nan recalled, "but shored up, like a mine tunnel. There were tunnels between buildings. It was very much like being in a mine. You had to climb out to see the sun."

Living quarters were cramped. In a space designed to house a small group of men who were there to do strenuous work,

Approaching the flat, polar plateau from the air, a traveler sees nothing but ice and snow in all directions.

Entrance to the old South Pole Station, as it appeared in 1974 when Nan Scott descended the "holy stairs"

there were no luxuries. Navy officials who had resisted the whole idea of including women in research at the Pole seemed most concerned about the lack of comfort and privacy. Nan and Donna didn't complain.

"The men were very considerate," Nan said. "They simply shared their facilities with us. The quarters building was divided into tiny rooms, on either side of a common hall. Donna and I shared a bunkroom. Down the hall there was a washroom with four sinks and toilets—like a school dormitory—and a single shower stall for everybody. No big problem. Just like sharing one bathroom with a big family of forty people. We managed."

Working space for the scientists was even more limited. The station, at that time, was still a U.S. Navy base. Its medical facility had been set up by Navy physicians for treating the men under their care.

"It was a good field station," Nan said, "but strictly for primary health care—never intended for the kind of research we wanted to do. There was an x-ray apparatus and a surgery suite with examining room and treatment room. It was adequate—but the lab was minimal."

The tiny laboratory, separate from the medical suite, was just a cubbyhole, four feet by four feet, furnished with a table and chair and shelves. The researchers found a microscope, a small refrigerator, and a little incubator, but no elaborate equipment.

"We had to work in the lab one at a time," Nan recalled. "There was no way for two people to fit into that room. One person could sit at the table in the middle of the lab and never need to get up. We didn't have everything we needed, but everything we *had* was within arm's reach. We had to do a lot of our work in other rooms, with makeshift equipment."

Dr. Muchmore remembers his frustration in those early years

when unexpected problems kept turning up and the work seemed to be taking twice as long as he expected.

"Everything takes longer at the Pole," he recalled. "Even brushing your teeth takes longer. Nobody who hasn't experienced it can quite imagine it. I didn't believe it at first—but now I know that it just takes more time and effort to do anything at the Pole—even simple tasks."

There were more serious problems, too. The Oklahoma scientists discovered that their biological culture medium was drying out in the lab. After all, they were in the middle of a desert. And it wasn't easy to keep everything sterile in a place where there was no water at all unless great quantities of snow were melted to produce it.

"Murphy's Law applies with a vengeance in the Antarctic," Muchmore said. "If anything can go wrong, it will. Every time we thought we were prepared for every kind of problem, something new turned up that we hadn't thought of. Everything has to be planned ahead of time. You have to take along whatever you think you're going to need. If you don't have it, you'll have to wait a full year before you can get it—then another year to get specimens. Time is a problem."

Muchmore and his team have come to expect the unexpected. No matter how much planning they do, they can always count on a few surprises. In the early years of the project, Nan Scott learned to cope with shortages and makeshift equipment. With endless patience, she repeated her laboratory tests over and over again. Then, in 1975, the new Amundsen-Scott South Pole Station was opened to replace the old ice-covered IGY station.

"What a difference!" Nan commented. "Our lab is superbly set up now. We've taken several seasons to set it up—duplicating as much as possible the equipment we use in Oklahoma. The

Amundsen-Scott South Pole Station, sheltered by a geodesic dome and two arches of corrugated steel

new lab is much bigger than the old one. Everything is more comfortable. We even have indoor-outdoor carpeting on the floors to make them warmer. They're still cold, but not as icy as they used to be. Dr. Muchmore says the old station had character, but the new station has class.''

At the height of the summer season—December and January—the new station houses eighty to a hundred people. Even in winter, when the temperature outside drops to a hundred degrees below zero, eighteen or twenty winter-over men and women are protected by the huge geodesic dome.

Under the dome you can walk around in relative comfort among the prefabricated buildings of a compact town—with suburbs a few yards away, under big steel arches that intersect the dome. Living quarters are just a few steps away from the science center, the post office and general store, or the red-carpeted dining room. You'll find the biomedical research building outside the dome, under one of the steel arches. A maintenance shop and generating plant are under another.

When you're not working, you may visit the gymnasium for a while or play a little ping-pong or find out which movie will be shown after dinner. If the washer-dryer is free, you can do your laundry. Or you can spend a quiet hour in the library— where the globe, you notice, shows the South Pole on top.

"We don't stay at the Pole for the whole season," Nan said. "Normally, we stay two or three weeks, then fly back to Oklahoma. We usually make a second trip in January—to get a late summer sampling of the winter-over people. Not everyone arrives at the same time. We go in on the first plane in October and a lot of the scientists don't come until December, so we'd miss a few winter-overs if we didn't return in mid-season. In January we take initial samples from the late arrivals and second samples from those we tested in November."

"Since her first trip to the Pole in 1973, Nan has missed only one season. That was in 1977–78 when she was completing her Ph.D. project. She had begun the work earlier, but had to miss classes every October—and again every January—when she traveled south. By skipping a year at the Pole she earned her doctorate in 1979 and was back on the job before the first flight in October.

"I'll keep on going back as long as the project continues," Nan said. "Obviously, I enjoy it. I love every minute of it. Besides, the lab work is very detailed and it's better to have the same person doing the tests, year after year. Continuity is important in this kind of work."

Test results have turned up several surprises during the first few years of the program. Some of them are challenging basic assumptions about the common cold and the viruses that cause it. One assumption has been that cold germs can't be transmitted from person to person in very cold, dry places like Antarctica. Or can they?

All of us carry germs in our noses and mouths, all the time, but we're ordinarily immune to our own germs. When someone else sneezes or coughs, we may be infected by their germs—unless our natural immunities are strong enough to fight the invading virus.

After long isolation at the Pole, people lose some of their immunities—but no new germs are brought in to infect them. Then, why do they catch cold in mid-season?

"This problem has intrigued me all along," Dr. Muchmore said. "At the Pole we usually see an outbreak of sniffles in the middle of the season—long after the ordinary incubation period has passed. There have been no planes in or out—no new germs have been imported—so where did the virus come from?"

Five years of research produced concrete evidence preserved in laboratory cultures—but medical researchers are cautious about making announcements.

"It's too early for conclusions," Nan said. "Everything takes more time in the Antarctic. If we observe a phenomenon one year, take another year to analyze the data, then go back to observe the same phenomenon again, we still have to analyze *that* data and make comparisons. It takes time. We have some specific theories—but we're not ready to make any claims."

In 1980 the Oklahoma team reported, very tentatively, that their evidence was "contrary to present concepts of respiratory virus epidemiology." They added that their research "may lead to revision of these concepts."

Women have participated in this project from the very beginning. Nan Scott and Donna Muchmore were the first. During the 1978–79 season, two other women, not formally associated with the Oklahoma project, took part in the testing. Dr. Marion Cooney, a Seattle virologist, and Dr. Michele Eileen Raney, a young physician from Los Angeles, arrived at the Pole with Dr. Muchmore and Dr. Scott.

For Dr. Cooney it was a brief visit. Her virus research at the University of Washington involved family surveillance studies in which she followed several families over a period of years, collecting specimens about every two weeks to see if any viruses were present. One of her cell cultures had been used by the Muchmore team in Antarctica for isolating virus specimens. In 1978 she was invited to go to the Pole to see what they were doing.

For Dr. Raney the experience was very different—unique— and crucial to the future role of women in Antarctica. The first

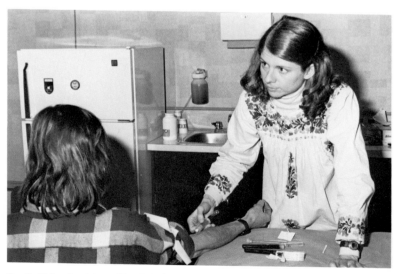

South Pole physician, Dr. Michele Raney, was the first woman to spend a full year at the bottom of the world.

woman ever selected—ahead of male applicants—to be year-round physician at the South Pole, she was also the first woman ever to spend a winter there. For a full year, this 27-year-old Californian was responsible for the medical welfare of the whole population.

The job was uniquely demanding. If it became necessary, she was expected to be surgeon, dentist, psychiatrist, and internist—as well as lab technician and nurse. At regular intervals, she collected blood samples and nasal washes for Dr. Muchmore's project.

When the year began, Dr. Raney seemed reluctant to talk about problems that could arise for a woman isolated with a group of men for such a long time. When it ended, she reported "no problems." Her most serious medical challenge had been an unexpected case of scurvy in a young man whose eating habits deprived him of necessary vitamins. There had been a few sprained ankles, the usual sniffles, and some teeth to be treated. Dr. Raney treated them. It was as simple as that.

Twelve

RADIATION
DETECTIVE

Like a giant dragonfly, a U.S. Navy helicopter hovers over the sandstone peaks that rise out of the ice in South Victoria Land. Inside the twin-engine aircraft, Gisela Dreschhoff focuses her attention on a steady stream of chart paper emerging from a gamma-ray spectrometer.

Intently, she watches the wavy red line made by a pen point that wiggles slightly as the paper moves under it. Dr. Dreschhoff is a radiation physicist, a specialist in detecting radioactive mineral deposits in rocks. The wavy line is her clue. If it should suddenly jump to a peak, she is ready to signal her companions.

Two pilots, occupying the front seats of the helicopter, keep their eyes on a changing horizon. Behind them, Gisela shares the limited space with Dr. Franz Tessensohn, a West German geophysicist who watches the landscape and keeps track of their location on a map.

At this moment, Gisela is the only one of the four passengers who seems unaware that the helicopter is heading straight for the side of a mountain. The pilot tenses his grasp of the controls—but doesn't change course.

"Close enough?" he asks.

Gisela Dreschhoff watches as a steady stream of chart paper emerges from the radiation detector.

Edward Zeller and Gisela Dreschhoff with gamma-ray spectrometer used to detect radioactive minerals

At a signal from Tessensohn, the pilot makes a skillful turn, just in time to avoid a crash, and steers the copter into a safe path close to the mountain face. Gisela's blue eyes never leave the chart paper.

In the austral summer of 1976-77, just a few months after receiving her U.S. citizenship papers, German-born Gisela was in Antarctica for the first time, searching for uranium. She would return again and again—to live and work in remote field camps, to do her share of hauling equipment and tunneling through snow, to spend endless hours in flight over unexplored mountaintops. Each new season would mean new adventures, but Gisela especially remembers that first year.

"We were starting a general radiometric survey," she explained. "We wanted to determine the distribution of uranium, thorium, and radioactive potassium—if there were any—in Antarctica."

Nothing like it had ever been tried before. Such surveys had been considered next to impossible in an area where ninety percent of the land is buried under ice—but Gisela and her colleagues were experimenting with a new system. It combined airborne surveys with on-the-ground measurements and made use of a gamma-ray spectrometer, a detection tool Gisela had used expertly since her student days in Germany.

Since 1972, when she became deputy director of the Radiation Physics Laboratory at the University of Kansas, Gisela had worked on radiometric surveys in the United States. Her colleague in the university's geology department, Professor Edward Zeller—an enthusiastic veteran of several seasons in Antarctica—invited Dr. Dreschhoff to join him, in 1976, on an international research project.

For the first season, the Kansas team consisted of three people—Dr. Zeller, Dr. Dreschhoff, and Kent Chrisler, a graduate student in the geology department. Their West German colleague, Dr. Tessensohn, offered his expertise as a geophysicist.

The scientists were not looking for a potential uranium mine. The Antarctic Treaty specifically forbids mining—at least while the treaty is in effect—but all the nations involved are trying to formulate a policy to govern future use of resources buried under the polar ice.

On a typical day the scientists spent hours flying over terrain where geologists thought uranium deposits might possibly be found. Usually, they found nothing worth following up. But sometimes the wavy red line on the chart paper jumped to sharp peaks, indicating stronger-than-normal radioactivity. When there were enough of these peaks in one place, the helicopter landed. On the ground, the scientists checked their findings with more precise instruments.

"In the helicopter," Gisela recalled, "we took turns watching the spectrometer. There were always two scientists in each airborne party. One of us would watch the terrain and direct the pilots while the other monitored the equipment."

Their detection tool was a huge crystal of sodium iodide, enclosed in an aluminum cylinder and fitted into an open space on the helicopter floor, between and slightly behind the two pilot seats. This was no ordinary crystal but an artificially cultivated lump of sodium iodide, measuring seven inches on a side. Even larger crystals were used in later surveys.

The crystal is a radiation detector, particularly sensitive to gamma rays. Radioactive minerals—such as uranium, thorium, and one form of potassium—give off gamma rays as they gradually decay. When a gamma ray hits the sodium iodide crystal, there is a tiny flash of light. In the gamma ray spectrometer, a light monitor detects the flash and jiggles the recording needle, causing a sudden peak on the chart paper. The higher the peak, the more gamma rays are coming out of the rock beneath the helicopter—so the scientists know that radioactive material is buried there.

Sometimes the Navy helicopter delivered the scientists to "promising" areas where radioactive deposits were expected.

When they land, the detection team can follow up these clues with a smaller hand-held spectrometer. They also carry a four-channel analyzer that gives them separate radiation counts for uranium, thorium, and potassium—as well as a total radiation count.

The first few weeks of the search were discouraging. Hours and hours of flying and chart-watching revealed no evidence of significant deposits. Then Gisela Dreschhoff made the first real find.

During a flight along the mountains that form the west wall

of the Beacon Valley, Gisela was conscientiously watching the chart paper, all but hypnotized by the monotony of the wavy red line. Suddenly, her vigilance paid off. The red line jumped to a peak so high that the needle swept off the chart. Gisela called to the pilot to turn back and fly over the area again.

For about a mile and a half, the radiation was almost three times the normal amount. This didn't indicate any huge deposits of uranium, but Dr. Zeller called it "the most encouraging find so far." He immediately made plans to follow up the discovery with investigation on the ground. The scientists collected specimens to be analyzed later in their laboratories at home.

"When the season ended," Gisela said, "people kept asking us if we had found any large deposits of uranium. We did not, of course, but we certainly were not disappointed. Our search was not intended to be a 'uranium hunt'—as the press called it—but a general survey. When you go into a survey of that kind you don't really expect to find anything in an area as limited as the one we surveyed. It would have been pure luck if we had found a large deposit."

After her first season in Antarctica, Gisela returned the following year to continue the survey. For six weeks during the 1977–78 season, she worked in Marie Byrd Land from a remote field camp known as Mabel One.

It was a small, temporary town about eight hundred miles from McMurdo. Five Jamesway huts had been airlifted to the spot and were set up on the ice to house about thirty-five people and three helicopters. Fifteen scientists from several universities, involved in a variety of research projects, shared the camp with an approximately equal number of U.S. Navy men—technicians, maintenance people, and helicopter pilots. The scientists took turns using the helicopters for daily field trips.

Gisela Dreschhoff at work in Antarctica

"For about a week," Gisela recalled, "the weather was beautiful and we made a few flights—but then there was a snowstorm. Within a few hours the whole camp was completely buried under snow. In the middle of the storm, the sun came out for a few hours. It was like the eye of a hurricane—calm and beautiful. During this break in the storm we dug a tunnel from one building to the next and covered it with plywood. We barely had time to finish the tunnel before the storm struck again—but after that we were able to move around comfortably within the camp—under the snow."

People who meet Gisela Dreschhoff for the first time in a non-polar setting—in Kansas or Washington or at some scientific meeting—find it difficult to imagine this slim young woman tunneling her way through an Antarctic snowbank. She looks deceptively fragile, with pale blonde hair and fair skin, wearing something very feminine in a size 8. If anyone expresses surprise that she is able to do such strenuous work, she shrugs.

"We are scientists. We do this kind of work because we want to do it. If you really want to do something, you usually find you can do it. Perhaps many women don't know what they are capable of doing."

Gisela has been testing her own capabilities since she was a child in Germany. Her training as a physicist, at the Technical University of Braunschweig, prepared her for an unusual career long before she ever dreamed of being a polar scientist. Her master's degree thesis on "The Determination of Radioactive Isotopes in Rocks by Gamma Ray Spectrometry" provided background that led her to a radiation laboratory in Kansas—and, eventually, to the Antarctic.

Gisela's first job made her a specialist in detecting low-level radiation. As a staff scientist at the German Federal Institute of Physics and Technology, she was involved in safety procedures to be used around nuclear reactors. In 1965, she was measuring the levels of radioactive fission products in German air, soil, water, and plants. Two years later, she attended a conference of the International Atomic Energy Agency in Monaco— a meeting that led to the opening of doors in unexpected places.

"At that meeting," she recalled later, "I met a number of American scientists. One of them, Professor Edward Zeller from the University of Kansas, was working on the effects of radiation on solid bodies in space. He had several contracts from the space program—from NASA and the Air Force—and was looking for a staff physicist. He offered me a job at the University of Kansas.

"It was a marvelous opportunity to work in America for a while, so I accepted. When I asked for a leave of absence from my job in Braunschweig, I really intended to stay away only one year. But when the year ended, I was enjoying the work so much that I asked for another half-year. After that, I had to make up my mind whether to go home to Germany or to stay in Kansas."

It wasn't an easy decision. Gisela missed her family and she had enjoyed the work in Braunschweig—but the space program was exciting and there seemed to be endless opportunities for her to do original work. She decided to stay in Kansas.

Gisela didn't waste time. She completed the requirements for her Ph.D. while working at the university as a research associate and then as visiting assistant professor in the department of physics and astronomy. By 1972 she was deputy director of the Radiation Physics Laboratory. Four years later she was on her way to Antarctica as a principal investigator, involved in an ambitious survey.

Because she speaks fluent German—as well as English and French—Gisela was a valuable participant in an international research project involving German scientists. Once the survey had begun, she returned to Antarctica every year, expecting to stay with the project for at least five years.

During this time she was "borrowed" by the National Science Foundation and spent a year in Washington as a research advisor in geophysics. In November, 1978, she flew to Antarctica as a representative of NSF, to coordinate airborne surveys for the entire geophysics program.

A huge cargo plane, the big LC-130 Hercules, was outfitted with equipment for several different kinds of research. There were cameras for aerial photography, antennas for radio echo sounding, a magnetometer for geomagnetism studies, and air-sampling equipment. Each project was directed by its own princi-

The physicists spent long hours flying over unexplored mountains.

pal investigators, but somebody had to decide who would use the plane on what days. That was Gisela's job.

"Suppose you have a flight scheduled to do air sampling," she said, "then the weather changes in the area where the sampling is to be done. What do you do? It's much too expensive to have the aircraft just sitting on the ground doing nothing. You want to use the time, so you change the schedule. Maybe the weather is better where the magnetic people want to go, so you schedule their flight instead."

Gisela not only scheduled the flights but also flew with the Hercules on some of the missions. Then she came to expect sleepless days and nights and learned to cope with unexpected delays and sudden changes in schedules.

"Sometimes we'd go to the runway, expecting to take off right away, and we'd have to wait for hours. A maintenance problem could delay several flights. Then, when we finally took off, we might be in the air for eighteen hours—so sometimes we didn't sleep for twenty-four hours at a stretch. I couldn't go on all the flights—I had to sleep sometimes—but I went on a lot of them."

At the end of that season Gisela returned to Washington, but by September, 1979, she was back in Kansas, preparing for another austral summer with the survey team in Antarctica. Once again she would work with the gamma-ray spectrometer aboard helicopters, taking off from a remote camp. This time the camp was in the Ellsworth Mountains.

The rugged Ellsworth Mountains are the highest in Antarctica with some peaks towering more than sixteen thousand feet. In this inhospitable area, Holmes and Narver construction workers set up a base camp. From McMurdo, ski-equipped Hercules planes made flight after flight, airlifting Jamesway huts, generators, tools, radio equipment, kitchen gear, and food for some fifty scientists.

When the researchers arrived, they swarmed over the mountains and glaciers—by helicopter and on foot—measuring, testing, mapping, examining everything from fossils in the rocks to movement of the ice. Gisela and her colleagues continued their systematic survey, searching for deposits of radioactive minerals.

To a layman, the job may seem overwhelming. The Antarctic

continent accounts for more than nine percent of all the land surface on earth. To make a complete survey of this huge area calls for years of tedious, demanding work—complicated by extremely hostile weather and winds, very high altitudes, and long distances between outcrops of ice-free rock. Detection devices won't work where the rock is covered by deep layers of ice. So, since much of Antarctica is buried under ice, the scientists sometimes fly for hours without gathering any useful information at all. It calls for patience.

At the end of the first three years of their survey, Gisela Dreschhoff and Edward Zeller estimated that they had measured radiation levels over about one-tenth of one percent of all the exposed rock in Antarctica. The work had just begun. In October, 1979, the Kansas radiation detectives reported their findings to an international symposium of nuclear scientists meeting in Buenos Aires.

"It is premature," they said, "to attempt any kind of comprehensive estimate of uranium resource potential of Antarctica."

They had discovered no big uranium deposits of commercial value, they said, but they had found deposits of thorium—and they had learned a great deal about the detailed geology of some parts of the great continent. They felt that their main achievement had been to demonstrate "that radiometric surveys can be performed successfully under the rigorous climatic conditions in Antarctica and that significant and reproducible data can be obtained."

As a scientist, Gisela finds the Antarctic work fascinating and rewarding. As a woman, she says she has never felt any discrimination at all. Her male colleagues have never made her feel less than equal.

"I can remember only one time when I wasn't quite sure

what to expect," she said. "That was in 1977–78 when we spent six weeks at the remote camp in Marie Byrd Land. I was the only woman there. When we landed, somebody pointed to one of the Jamesways and said, 'Sleeping quarters for the scientists are over there.' So we picked up our bags and walked over. Inside the building we found a row of little cots lined up along the wall. As we went in, everybody chose a cot. When it was my turn, I chose mine. Nobody made any comments. Nobody raised an eyebrow. We simply did our work."

That same year, Gisela had another experience shared by very few people in the world. At the South Pole she took her turn at pulling a sled loaded with three hundred pounds of equipment. "Manhauling" was a common practice in the old days of Antarctic exploration—before the advent of helicopters, tractors, snowmobiles, and ski-equipped cargo planes. Today it is seldom necessary, except in protected areas where motor vehicles are not allowed.

"Near Pole Station there is an area set aside for very clean operations," Gisela explained. "Motor vehicles would contaminate the air and snow, so anything that goes into the area has to be carried on foot or by sled. We had to load our heavy equipment onto a sled and pull it about a mile across the ice. That would be easy at sea level, but at an altitude of nine thousand feet, it's hard work."

The scientists were there to measure levels of radioactive fallout in the snow, using their gamma-ray detector crystal. Whenever nuclear weapons are tested in the atmosphere, anywhere in the world, radioactive debris may come down anywhere on the globe. At the South Pole, this fallout is preserved in the snow and can be measured years after the explosion that created it.

Gisela Dreschhoff did her share of hauling the heavy sled.

This time the Kansas team included two women, Gisela and a graduate student, Karen Harrower. They "womanhauled" the heavy sled and helped to lower the detector into a pit thirty feet deep.

"The pit was already there, so we didn't have to dig it," Gisela said. "It had been dug by French scientists earlier in the year, but we had to climb in and out of it all day, taking measurements. We had been told to expect altitude sickness. Some people really suffer for a couple of days after they land at the Pole—but I never felt any sickness at all. We really didn't have time. We started to work the day after we arrived."

For seven hours, that first day, the researchers worked in the cold wind, climbing in and out of the pit. Then they loaded their equipment on the sled and hauled it back to the station.

"We were tired," Gisela recalled, "but we had done a day's

work. We were sitting in the mess hall, waiting for dinner to begin, when two huge construction workers came in and collapsed in chairs near us. They were talking about how exhausted they were and how hard they had worked and how cold and windy it had been."

Gisela and Karen half-listened to the conversation. One of the men complained that he really couldn't stand it for very long.

"How long were you out there?" asked the other.

"Twenty minutes," was the reply.

The two women looked at each other and smiled. Weak women?

"I don't let anybody tell me that," Gisela said.

Thirteen

CATCH A
FALLING STAR

If you find a meteorite, *don't* put it in your pocket. "Hands off!" is the rule for Antarctic geologists—or for anyone else who happens to find one of these unearthly rocks lying on the polar ice.

By analyzing meteorite samples, scientists can learn a great deal about other planets and moons and the materials that make up the universe. But a space sample contaminated by earthly germs is less useful.

"Your first impulse is to pick it up and take a closer look," said Ursula Marvin. "Don't do it. The meteorites we find in Antarctica are of extraordinary importance to science. Fortunately for us, they fell into the cleanest and most sterile environment on earth, so we're doing our best to keep them uncontaminated."

Dr. Marvin, a meteoritist at the Smithsonian Astrophysical Observatory in Cambridge, Massachusetts, knows the rules. She was one of the scientists consulted by the National Aeronautics and Space Administration about procedures for handling moon rocks brought back by the *Apollo* astronauts. She is also a member

Ursula Marvin found meteorites on the ice.

of the committee that makes rules for handling Antarctic meteorites.

She knows the excitement of discovery—and the temptation to pick up the specimens she finds. During the 1978–79 research season in Antarctica, she was part of an international team searching for meteorites on the ice.

Why Antarctica? "Nowhere else in the world are so many

different kinds of meteorites found together in one place," Dr. Marvin explained. "In Antarctica—just in the past few years—investigators from Japan and the United States have found specimens of all classes of meteorites—stone, iron and stony-iron—and some varieties of stones never seen before."

Meteors have been a source of wonder on earth since early humans first noticed streaks of light in the sky that seemed to be falling stars. Now scientists believe they are grains of dust released from comets. As they fall through the earth's atmosphere, these small particles of rock or metal create friction and heat up until they glow. During their brief, bright journey they are meteors. Meteorites are something else.

"Once in a while," Ursula Marvin explained, "a large fragment enters the atmosphere and creates a spectacular fireball that streaks to earth accompanied by thunderous explosions. Molten droplets fly off in a fiery trail. If such a body is large enough to survive flight through the atmosphere, it may either collide with the earth as a single object or explode above the surface, falling as a shower of metal or rock fragments. Either way, once they reach the ground, they are called meteorites."

They can fall anywhere on earth, but the polar ice cap is a unique collecting ground. For thousands of years the ice has been a natural storage vault, not only preserving these specimens from space but somehow shifting and moving them into concentrated collections. In some places, the surface ice evaporates and leaves meteorites exposed, just waiting to be found.

"I couldn't believe it," Ursula said. "One afternoon right after lunch, there were three of us working in the field—one Japanese and two Americans. We were on a steep, icy slope and we began finding meteorites. Before the afternoon was over we had found twenty-three specimens.

"That doesn't mean twenty-three different meteorites," she explained. "If a meteorite breaks into hundreds or thousands of pieces in the atmosphere, all of the fragments in a shower are counted as a single meteorite. We couldn't know, until we had studied our specimens carefully, just how many different meteorites were represented. But we could tell that twenty-one of our specimens were the same general size and shape, the same color, with the same degree of weathering. We could make a preliminary guess that they were all part of the same fall. Two others were distinctly different—obviously not parts of the same body. So we knew we had found parts of two meteorites—or maybe three—but not twenty-three."

During a single six-week season, Ursula and her colleagues collected more than three hundred specimens. Each bit of rock was handled with meticulous care—picked up with sterile tools and put into sterile Teflon bags like those used by the *Apollo* astronauts for packaging moon samples.

"We go out with a whole backpack full of collecting equipment," Ursula said. "NASA supplies a lot of it. Along with the Teflon bags, we have a bunch of aluminum tags, prestamped with numbers in sequence, and a numbering device to use in photographs, showing a scale in centimeters. The same equipment was used for the lunar rocks."

Her enthusiasm grows as she describes a typical meteorite "capture."

"There you are on the ice. It's cold. The wind is blowing, your nose is running, you're wearing very dark glasses, and you think you see something that might be a meteorite. What you want to do is pick the thing up and examine it. But you can't do that. You have to kneel down or even lie down on the ice and get a better look. Most of the pictures of me that were taken out there show me face down on the ice.

"If you're still uncertain about the rock, reach for your pocket lens and examine it. Some meteorites are obvious and some are not. If you decide this one is probably a meteorite, you take out the numbering device, rack up the next number in your sequence of aluminum tags, set the device down next to the rock, then photograph it."

This picture-taking process is important. Each member of an international exploring party wants to record the find in several photographs—for a national organization, perhaps for a university, and, of course, for a personal record.

Don't touch the meteorites! Stony Meteorite Number 386 was packaged in a sterile Teflon bag after being photographed.

After a specimen has been thoroughly photographed, the scientists try to maneuver it into a Teflon bag without touching it. Then they tape it up and put it into a second bag with one of the numbered aluminum tags, allowing the tag to show through.

"That's just the beginning," Ursula continued. "We not only collect them clean, we keep them frozen. They're shipped to California in the freezer locker of a ship, then flown to Houston, still frozen, and are received at NASA's Johnson Space Center. NASA volunteered to accept and curate the Antarctic meteorite samples, just as they did the lunar rocks."

In the Houston lab the rocks are unpackaged—very carefully, one by one, inside a "glove box" filled with dry nitrogen. They are photographed again and assigned a new number. NASA scientists do a preliminary study of each specimen before repackaging it and storing it with the others in a germ-free cabinet.

"They usually take off a chip," Ursula said, "and send it to the Smithsonian for a thin section and a quick description. The point is to get well-documented information out, as soon as possible, to researchers around the world. Whenever a batch of specimens has been processed, a newsletter is sent out, telling them what kind of research material is available. The newsletter describes the hand specimen, the thin section, and any chemical analysis that has been done. We do just a little preliminary work—not too much. Nobody wants to work on a meteorite if somebody back in the original lab did too much on it."

Meteorite scientists compete for the privilege of working on the Antarctic specimens. They're eager to find out what the rocks are made of, how old they are, where they came from.

For some scientists the most fascinating question of all is, "Do they contain any evidence of life?" The samples these researchers want to study are extremely rare carbonaceous chondrites—rich in hydrocarbons and water and so soft that they leave black smudges on hands and paper.

According to Dr. Marvin, "They are the most primitive and least changed of any specimens available to us. Their chemical composition resembles that of the body of the sun. We've known for years that Type I carbonaceous chondrites contain organic hydrocarbons and all the elements essential to living organisms. When amino acids were first found in such meteorites, there was a lot of excitement. Now these molecules have been identified in at least one Antarctic specimen. They are definitely compounds of extra-terrestrial origin. When these amino acids were dissolved in solutions, they showed optical properties opposite to those of amino acids originating on earth."

There also has been some misunderstanding. Words like "organic" and "amino acid" led to false assumptions among nonscientists. There were reports of "evidence of life" found on the meteorites. Ursula Marvin is ready to clear away the confusion.

"So far, we haven't found any living material in these samples," she said. "We've never found any evidence that the hydrocarbons were ever part of living material. Organic and inorganic are not very precise definitions. Organic doesn't always mean biologic—or living. But these samples do show us hydrocarbon compounds that existed in the solar system before the advent of life. From them we gain insight into the processes that led to the origin of life on earth."

The failure—so far—to find living material on meteorite samples does not mean that scientists have given up hope of finding it. In laboratories all over the world researchers are applying more and more sophisticated techniques to their study of meteorites. A specialist like Ursula Marvin finds this exciting—and she always keeps an open mind.

She calls herself "an old-fashioned, romantic field geologist with a lot of wanderlust," but the thought of becoming a geologist didn't enter her mind until her junior year at Tufts College, in the 1940s.

"I never meant to be a scientist at all," she confided, years later, to a group of young women considering careers in space science. "All the way through high school I believed I had no aptitude for it. In those days, to get a humanities degree, you had to take two full years of elementary sciences. As a freshman I took biology and disliked it so intensely that, if only one year of science had been required, that would have been my brush with science forever. I put off the second science course until my junior year—and it was geology. That subject lighted a fire within two or three weeks. By that time, I knew what I would like to do—if I could."

As a senior, Ursula took every geology course she could manage, then received a B.A. in history. After that she was as single-minded as an Olympic athlete. A master's degree in geology from Harvard University, in 1946, was her gold medal. Her Ph.D. was postponed twenty-three years. Time out for wander-lust.

In the 1950s, Ursula and her geologist husband, Tom Marvin, hiked through remote areas of South America and Africa, field-mapping and searching for mineral ores. In the 1960s she returned to Harvard, began studying meteorites, and became a staff geologist at the Smithsonian Astrophysical Observatory.

"It was an ideal time for a geological-mineralogical background to be applied to the space sciences," she recalled. "The Apollo astronauts were about to land on the moon for the first time. They were going to bring back the first samples of lunar rocks and we couldn't wait to start working on them. Investigators in at least ten countries were working on new techniques for analyzing tiny samples."

The first of several collections of moon rocks arrived on earth in 1969. That was a memorable year for Ursula Marvin. She received her Ph.D. from Harvard, but the satisfaction of becoming "Dr. Marvin" was almost forgotten in the excitement she shared with other space scientists over three other events.

Early that year, on February 8, a spectacular fireball exploded in the atmosphere and showered thousands of pieces over Puebelito de Allende in Mexico. Scientists identified the meteorite as a carbonaceous chondrite. An exciting find. And there were plenty of samples available—enough to send to all the researchers who wanted to study them.

In July, the *Apollo 11* team landed on the moon and collected enough samples of rocks and soil to keep space geologists busy for years. Then in December—an appropriate ending for a year of discovery—Japanese glaciologists came upon an unusual collection of meteorites in Antarctica.

The scientists were working on the ice cap in the Yamato Mountains when a surveyor's chain caught on a rock. One of the researchers recognized the rock as a meteorite. Once they started looking, the men found eight more specimens nearby. When these samples were analyzed, the discoverers were amazed to find out that they were of several different varieties—obviously from five or six different meteorite falls.

It was extremely unusual to find different kinds of meteorites so close together. The first discovery had been accidental, but during three later field seasons Japanese scientists made a systematic search. They collected an unbelievable 992 specimens, probably representing at least a hundred different falls. Antarctica, it seemed, was a unique hunting ground for meteorite scientists.

By 1976, American scientists had begun searching near McMurdo, on the opposite side of the continent from the Yamato Mountains. Dr. William A. Cassidy of the University of

Pittsburgh's Department of Earth and Planetary Sciences led the first U.S. team. During five Antarctic summers, he directed a joint search in which Japanese and American teams worked as partners.

Ursula Marvin was very much aware of all these developments. At the Smithsonian Astrophysical Observatory she worked on moon rocks from the time *Apollo 11* returned in 1969. In 1973 she spent three months in Houston as part of the preliminary examination team for *Apollo 17* samples. Later she returned to Houston as a member of a NASA planning team, outlining procedures for analyzing the lunar specimens. As president of the Meteoritical Society in 1975–76, she was in touch with Antarctic researchers and fascinated by their discoveries.

Dr. William A. Cassidy of the University of Pittsburgh directed a joint search for meteorites, in cooperation with Japanese scientists.

"In October, 1977," she recalled, "I was invited to Washington for an NSF conference on Antarctic meteorites. We met to discuss the meteorites—to agree on some guidelines, to decide how samples should be handled. It had become quite an issue. It was difficult to think of all the problems that might arise without actually being in the field myself. Besides, I had always wanted to go to Antarctica—so I asked how to go about it."

A year later she was on her way to the ice, a member of William Cassidy's team of meteorite hunters. Their Japanese colleagues, including Dr. Kazuyuki Shiraishi, joined them at McMurdo. During the brief six-week season, Ursula had a chance to sample two very different field camps.

"There was a big temporary camp at Darwin Glacier," she said, "too far away from McMurdo for daily trips by helicopter. By Antarctic standards, the camp was huge. At least fifteen groups worked out of there during the season. We had all the necessities—a galley, a cook, a radio shack, a stretch of uncrevassed ice for landing Hercules aircraft, a helicopter pad, and a fuel dump. Our dormitory was a big Jamesway hut.

"Every day, if the weather permitted, we went out by helicopter. Sometimes we'd use the helicopter for reconnaisance. If you fly at about eight meters, you can see rocks fairly clearly—even little ones, about two centimeters across. You can easily recognize concentrations that might be meteorites."

Sometimes the helicopter would leave the meteoritists in the field for a day—always with extra survival equipment. The scientists stored their extra tent and food in a cache near the landing spot, then worked on foot—always keeping within sight of each other.

"There was some sitting around at Darwin, waiting for the weather to clear," Ursula remembered. "While I was there, I

From a tiny camp in the Allan Hills, Ursula Marvin and her colleagues went out by snowmobiles to search for meteorites.

was the only woman scientist—but now and then another woman turned up as part of a helicopter crew."

After about two weeks at the Darwin Glacier camp, Ursula and Shiraishi flew out to the remote Allan Hills where Cassidy was already at work. That was a very different kind of camp—just tents on the ice for three scientists.

"We had an extra tent," she recalled, "so I had the luxury of a private tent. I really appreciated that—after the dormitory at Darwin.

"Every day we went out on snowmobiles. I had one of my own. Shiraishi had a Japanese vehicle and Cassidy had a larger one, carrying equipment. We'd start out in separate directions. If one of us found a meteorite, we just had to stop and wait until the others noticed our signal. Then they'd come roaring up on their snowmobiles and we'd photograph the rock several times and go through the whole procedure with the Teflon bags."

Ursula's colleagues have a favorite story to tell about their first female teammate. On her very first day in the field, they said, she turned out to be the fastest treasure hunter around. Within fifteen minutes, she had found a meteorite as big as a football.

"It's true," Ursula laughed. "It was an accident—but, yes, I found a meteorite right away. The helicopter had just dropped us in the field for the day at a site that was crowded with other rocks—dark-colored basalts. I had an ice ax and was turning over some rocks, so I'd know what the common rocks were. I did that to two or three rocks. They were all basalts. Then I caught my crampon on another rock and fell on it. When I turned it over, I could see it was a meteorite.

"Well, I had already broken the rules. After I had fallen on it, the specimen was contaminated—so I picked it up and carried it around in amazement. Here was just the kind of rock you're always afraid you'll miss—a meteorite that didn't look like one."

That season, while Ursula searched for rocks that had fallen from space, a Florida microbiologist was looking for another kind of Antarctic rock. Her discoveries in the dry valleys led to new speculations about life on other planets.

Fourteen

MARTIAN
GARDEN

Is there life on Mars? Until the first earthlings actually walk across the rocky martian plains, nobody can be sure what they'll find there, but Roseli Ocampo Friedmann offers a few clues. She has found primitive life forms in the Antarctic desert, Earth's most hostile environment. Is Mars any more hostile?

According to some space scientists, the martian landscape may resemble the dry valleys of Antarctica.

"It may or may not be a very close resemblance," Roseli Ocampo explained, "but it's the closest we have on Earth. Mars is a cold, dry desert. Antarctica is the coldest, driest place on Earth—so the microbiology of the Antarctic dry valleys may tell us something about martian life, if it exists. We haven't yet looked inside the rocks of Mars."

Inside the rocks? If that sounds farfetched, take a look at Dr. Ocampo's laboratory at Florida State University in Tallahassee, where rows and rows of test tubes and Petri dishes contain living cultures of blue-green algae found growing inside desert rocks.

"Roseli has a blue-green thumb," says her husband and co-researcher, Dr. Imre Friedmann. "These organisms grow very, very slowly in nature. It may take months—or sometimes years— to see any growth at all. But Roseli can fatten them up in the laboratory so we can see them develop and learn more about them."

The two microbiologists have been working with desert algae since 1963, soon after Imre Friedmann discovered minute colonies of these microorganisms living inside rocks of the Negev Desert in Israel.

"A geologist friend, Dr. Eliazer Kashai, brought me a rock he had found in the Negev," Dr. Friedmann recalled. "When he cracked it open, it showed something green inside. The green was not copper and he wondered if it might be some biological material. We examined it in the lab and discovered there were tiny one-celled organisms inside. They were algae. Then we went out into the desert and found more such rocks."

Before that, algae had always been associated with water. Nobody had suspected that desert rocks could sustain life. Still, the Friedmanns do not claim the discovery entirely for themselves.

"Every scientific discovery has a predecessor," Imre Friedmann said, "and the predecessor has a predecessor. We looked through old literature and found an overlooked item. Somebody actually saw algae inside rocks in the European Alps in 1914. But," he added, "I think the discovery of algae inside *desert* rocks is ours."

When he made this startling find, Professor Friedmann was teaching at the Hebrew University in Jerusalem. Roseli Ocampo, a graduate student just arrived from the Philippines, was looking for a topic for her master's degree thesis. Fascinated by her professor's discovery, she asked if she might try to grow some

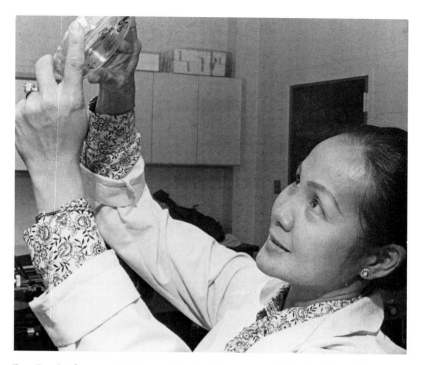

Dr. Roseli Ocampo Friedmann in the laboratory at Florida State University, Tallahassee

of the microscopic algae in laboratory cultures. The organisms grew—and became part of a pioneer research project.

The first formal announcement of the discovery of algae living inside desert rocks was made by the Friedmann team in 1964. Their paper, presented to the Fifth International Botanical Congress in Edinburgh, stirred up no excitement.

"It was accepted as just one of those odd facts of nature," Friedmann recalled. "Maybe some people wondered if it were really true."

Two years later, with a master's degree in biology, Roseli Ocampo returned to the Philippines. At the National Institute of Science and Technology in Manila, she resumed her earlier work. It involved microscopic examinations of pond water, where milkfish fed and were caught, to record periodic changes in the quality and quantity of algae, the principal diet of milkfish. Roseli's tests were especially important in a part of the world where milkfish are a popular food, but she missed the excitement she had known in Jerusalem. Pond algae provided only a mild substitute for the feeling of discovery she had found inside the desert rocks.

After making up her mind to go back to school for a Ph.D., she wrote to her mentor, Professor Friedmann, and asked his advice. By that time, Imre Friedmann had moved to Canada, and then to the United States. At Florida State University in Tallahassee he was continuing the work with desert algae and was planning to collect more specimens in Death Valley. He approved of Roseli's idea for a doctoral dissertation on desert algae. Would she like to expand her work with the cultures?

"She decided to do comprehensive work on desert algae for her thesis," Imre Friedmann remembered. "It was an important and voluminous work which required a great deal of skill and patience. The work was based on cultures which she grew in her laboratory—from organisms found in hot deserts all over the world. The result of that culture collection exists now at Florida State University. It serves as the basis for that part of our research supported by NASA."

Before 1976, Roseli Ocampo was Mrs. Imre Friedmann—although Ocampo remained her professional name. Their joint research had attracted the attention of the National Aeronautics and Space Administration, because of its implications for space biology. Since NASA was already supporting other research in Antarctica, the Friedmanns eventually moved their search for life in the rocks from hot deserts to the coldest desert of all.

For several years the American space program had used the dry valleys of Antarctica as a testing ground for various theories about Mars. In 1976 the Viking spacecraft were being prepared for their interplanetary journey. Complex electronic instruments were being designed and programmed to carry out experiments on the surface of Mars. In the early 1970s, space scientists tried out some of the experiments in Antarctica.

As early as 1969, microbiologists involved in the Mars project had collected and analyzed Antarctic soil samples, searching for primitive life forms. They found a few microbes, but by 1973 they concluded that these organisms had not originated in Antarctica. Probably, they said, microbes had been carried by the winds from more temperate places. They were not convinced that Antarctica had any native microbial life at all.

Roseli Ocampo and Imre Friedmann read about these conclusions with interest—and some impatience. They had a laboratory full of proof that microscopic plants could live inside the rocks of hot deserts. Why didn't somebody look beneath the surface of Antarctic rocks? They wanted to go to Antarctica and see for themselves, but the possibility seemed unlikely.

"It wasn't easy to get financial support for such a far-out idea as ours," Roseli recalled. "After all, we wanted to look for organisms in a place where other microbiologists had said nothing could live."

They began their Antarctic research without going to Antarctica. A colleague, Dr. Wolf Vishniac, a microbiologist from the University of Rochester, was deputy leader of the biology team of Project Viking, the Mars mission. He was going to Antarctica for the 1973–74 season to continue a search for life in the dry valley soil. Friedmann asked Vishniac to bring back some rock samples.

A few months later, the Friedmanns received disturbing news. Vishniac was dead. While climbing a steep and rocky Antarctic slope, the biologist had slipped and fallen to his death.

Vishniac's research ended abruptly and the Friedmanns set aside their plans for studying Antarctic rocks. Then, nearly a year later, they received a letter from Helen Vishniac, their friend's widow. Before his tragic accident, her husband had not forgotten his promise to collect samples for his Florida colleagues. Mrs. Vishniac, herself a microbiologist, recognized the importance of the rocks he had collected. She packed them up and sent them to Tallahassee.

Primitive life forms—bacteria—found inside Antarctic rocks, magnified 38,000 times by scanning electron microscope

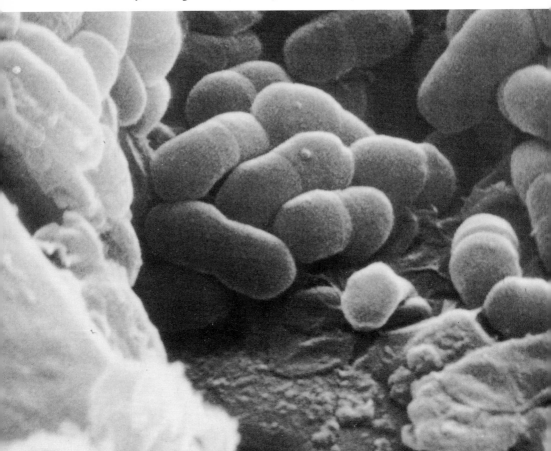

"In one of the rocks," Roseli recalled, "we did find a very clear growth—very much like the ones we had found in hot deserts."

Roseli transferred some of the green material from the rock to culture dishes. After some eleven weeks and a lot of patience, she could see that the microscopic cells had begun to grow.

Based on their findings in this single sample, Roseli Ocampo and Imre Friedmann submitted a joint paper to *Science,* reporting their discovery of living algae under the surface of Antarctic rock. They suggested that scientists who were looking for extra-terrestrial life might consider the possibility of endolithic (within-rock) life forms on Mars.

The paper appeared in the September 24 issue of *Science,* 1976. That was the year when NASA's two Viking spacecraft had landed on Mars to scoop up samples of martian soil and test it for evidence of life. No conclusive proof had been found, but scientists were still debating their conflicting interpretations of the results.

Some NASA scientists were intrigued by the Friedmanns' suggestion. Suppose there *were* some form of life inside the martian rocks. Viking instruments, programmed to test soil only from the surface, could have overlooked it—just as earlier researchers in Antarctica had overlooked the blue-green algae inside dry valley rocks. The idea seemed worth pursuing.

By this time the Friedmanns had received a grant from the National Science Foundation to continue their Antarctic investigations. As members of the United States Antarctic Research Program, they could now search for their own specimens of rock-dwelling algae in Antarctica. For the first two seasons, Roseli stayed in the Tallahassee laboratory while her husband collected rock samples in the dry valleys. She prepared the cultures and waited for their strange garden to grow.

There were difficulties. By the time Roseli received the rocks and was able to transfer some of the blue-green growth to her culture vials, they had traveled thousands of miles in all kinds of weather. During the long trip from Antarctica to Florida, many of the organisms had been damaged.

"We realized then," she explained, "that it was important for me to be there, too—on the spot. If I could begin the cultures immediately, as soon as the samples were brought in from the field, there would be less danger of contamination or damage."

By 1978 she was out in the field with her husband, armed with a geology pick and a large supply of sterile plastic bags. By 1980 she was an Antarctic veteran.

When she is collecting samples in Antarctica, Roseli works out of McMurdo, making daily trips by helicopter to the dry valleys. A typical day begins very early in the morning. Before each trip she spends about an hour in the biology laboratory, sterilizing glass vials and carefully measuring the culture medium that will nourish the day's collection of microscopic specimens. Once the vials are prepared, she is ready to board the helicopter.

Roseli and Imre Friedmann usually go together on these collecting trips. They know exactly what they are looking for. Rocks most likely to contain organisms are usually translucent or porous enough to allow some light to seep in. Even the most primitive life forms need light for photosynthesis.

When they find rocks that look promising, the Friedmanns break them up with a pick and take a closer look. If there is a dark, greenish stripe just under the surface, they know they have uncovered part of a hidden microworld.

Very carefully, Roseli brings out the sterile plastic bags and starts packaging pieces of rock. She seals each bag and marks it with a felt-tip pen to show the date and location of the find.

Roseli and Imre Friedmann carefully package samples of rock containing microscopic life.

Roseli notes the exact location of an endolithic colony.

At the end of the day, the helicopter picks up the Florida scientists and takes them back to McMurdo. But Roseli's work is not yet finished. She goes at once to the laboratory.

Without removing a rock from its sterile package, she breaks it up with a hammer. Then, with sterile forceps, she removes a tiny bit of rock and very carefully puts it into the sterilized culture medium. When all the vials are filled she prepares them for the journey to Florida, packing them with dry ice in a specially insulated container. After that, she takes no chances with the precious package. It travels with her, never out of sight, until she lands in Tallahassee.

In the university laboratory, the Antarctic section of Roseli's microbial garden grows in a big refrigerator. She keeps the temperature as close as possible to the dry-valley environment—about four degrees Centigrade. For some specimens she changes conditions to speed up their growth. She may change the temperature, the amount of light, or the composition of the growth medium—or all three. This way, the Friedmanns can keep an eye on gradual changes that might take many years in nature—watching them happen over a period of months.

"We are finding answers to some of our questions about these organisms," Roseli said, "but some very specific questions can't be answered in the laboratory—yet. We want to know more about conditions inside the rocks. Exactly how much light gets in? How much water exists there? What are the temperature limits of these microorganisms? What chemical changes take place inside the rock because these organisms are there? We know there *is* an effect. They do something to the rock—but what?"

These questions, the Friedmanns believe, can be answered in Antarctica—with the help of some very sophisticated electronic equipment. Tiny sensors, inserted into rocks and connected to recording devices, can be left in place for days at a time to measure changes of temperature and humidity at different depths inside the rock.

This very precise new phase of their work began during the 1979-80 season. The program grew more ambitious—and international—when scientists from West Germany and Israel joined the Friedmann team. By 1981 they would be ready to move from the dry valleys to other areas of Antarctica, so far unexplored by microbiologists.

Roseli is cautious about making predictions. She knows how suddenly plans can change.

"We are at the mercy of the weather in Antarctica," she said. "Mechanical breakdowns, too, can change all our plans."

She accepts the uncertainty now, but it wasn't so easy when she made her first trip to Antarctica. Imre was already there and she was impatient to join him. As soon as she finished her classroom teaching for the year, she set out for New Zealand. After a day in Christchurch she had been outfitted with Antarctic clothing and was ready to leave for McMurdo.

On the day of the flight she reported to the airbase before daylight, expecting to see her husband that afternoon. Two weeks later, she was still in Christchurch. Eight times she boarded the plane and watched New Zealand disappear in the distance. Three times, the big Starlifter traveled halfway to McMurdo; then the weather turned stormy and the pilot had to turn back. Five more attempts to cover the distance ended even sooner. Each time, Roseli had to get up before dawn and check in at the airbase. After the ninth check-in, they finally made it.

Between trips to Antarctica, Roseli keeps up with a busy schedule in Tallahassee. In addition to her work as a principal investigator at Florida State University, she is also on the faculty of Florida A and M University where she teaches courses in cell biology, microbiology, and general biology. No matter how busy she is, she always keeps a protective eye on her laboratory garden of desert algae.

"It is absolutely unique," says her husband, proudly. "Roseli's culture collection is the only collection of this sort in the world. Here we have a collection of organisms that live and adapt themselves to extreme environments by particular properties that other organisms do not possess. We are trying to find out what is the basis of their resistance to harsh environments. What peculiar mechanisms are present? Eventually, we would like to make the collection available to other investigators, all over the world."

Fifteen

FIRE
AND ICE

Inside the main crater of Mount Erebus, an icy wind whipped back the hood of Katharine Cashman's parka. In December, 1978, she was at work on the summit of Antarctica's most spectacular volcano. From a small camp near the rim, she had just climbed down three hundred feet to the main crater floor.

"It was a new and mysterious world," she recalled. "Steaming vertical cliffs rising on all sides, the ground covered with volcanic bombs—some of them seven feet across. We could see a gaping hole in the crater floor. That was the inner crater, plunging another four hundred feet down."

A few days before Christmas, Kathy and five companions, peering through clouds of steam that rose from the inner crater, their faces flushed from the heat, were operating a system of ropes and pulleys. At the other end of the ropes, Dr. Werner Giggenbach slowly and carefully descended the almost veritcal inner wall—closer and closer to a pulsating lake of molten lava.

Slowed down by layers of insulated clothing, he moved very deliberately, like a bear climbing down a tree trunk. A gas mask protected his lungs from poisonous volcanic fumes, and a two-way radio kept him in touch with his colleagues on the rim.

Dr. Giggenbach, a geochemist with New Zealand's Department of Scientific and Industrial Research (DSIR), was aiming toward the floor of the inner crater. If he made it, he would be the first person ever to set foot on that part of the earth. There, close to their source, he hoped to collect samples of hot gases emitted by the lava. These gases, the driving force behind all volcanic eruptions, might provide answers to fundamental questions about the earth's chemical make-up.

Kathy, very much aware of the movement in the lava lake, kept an anxious eye on Dr. Giggenbach.

"It was like a huge pot of porridge," she said. "The molten lava moved continuously. Now and then the black surface was broken by flashes of red when bubbles burst—revealing the hot lava below—then hardened, immediately, to form a thin black crust. All the while there was an eerie hissing from the steam vents."

The ropes slackened for a moment as Dr. Giggenbach paused, about four-fifths of the way down. Bracing himself, he reached out to untangle his lifeline. Suddenly, without warning, the volcano erupted in a blinding flash. A shower of debris—including lava bombs as big as footballs—rained down into the crater.

"Nobody in the main crater was hurt," Kathy said, "but our main concern was for Werner Giggenbach. We were relieved when he answered our call on the walkie-talkie. He was okay. He didn't even seem upset. Werner's pretty cool, but we were afraid the ropes might have been damaged—that had happened before—so we pulled him up. He had been hit by a small piece of debris that burned a hole in the knee of his pants, but it didn't go through his long underwear."

Katharine Cashman watched a volcano erupt in Antarctica.

Kathy's recollection of the event seemed equally cool. "It wasn't as scary as it sounds," she said. "The explosion reminded me of a bomb going off in a war movie. Most of the bombs went straight up—then fell almost straight down. We had time to dodge the bits of lava as they fell."

For Katharine Cashman of Rumford, Rhode Island, it was a new experience—getting acquainted with an Antarctic volcano. Little more than a year earlier, the whole idea had been undreamed-of. It wasn't surprising that she was studying to be a geologist—with a grandfather, an uncle, and two sisters already in the profession—but there were no vulcanologists among them.

After graduation from Middlebury College in Vermont, Kathy had received a Fullbright Fellowship for graduate study in geology. While working toward a master's degree at Victoria University in Wellington, New Zealand, she had discovered the fascination of volcanoes.

The North Island of New Zealand is a paradise for vulcanologists. From all over the world, they come to study the island's volcanoes or to observe thermal springs and geysers. For many of them, the geology building on the campus of Victoria University becomes headquarters. Students like Kathy often share laboratory space with the world's experts. She heard a great deal of talk about volcano research and about the adventures of New Zealanders exploring the hot crater of an active volcano surrounded by Antarctic ice.

Soon after her arrival in Wellington, Kathy knew she wanted to study vulcanology. She also thought about the Antarctic.

"When you look at the map," she said, "New Zealand looks so close to Antarctica. It is—relatively close. All the American planes take off from New Zealand when they're going to the Antarctic. So I started asking around. I thought maybe I could go down and just look around. But it wasn't as easy as I had supposed. You have to be part of an official scientific research project if you want to travel around the continent. I was just a student—so I gave up hope. Besides, I was working hard to finish my thesis on a volcanic area of the central North Island."

At the end of her first year in Wellington, Kathy returned to Rhode Island for Christmas with her family. By February, 1978, she was back in New Zealand organizing a field trip.

February is late summer in the Southern Hemisphere—like August in the northern half. In downtown Wellington, shoppers in shirt sleeves and summer dresses sometimes looked up at the craggy silhouette of Victoria University's old stone buildings perched on a sun-baked cliff. Some of the shoppers were Antarctic scientists, returning to—or passing through—New Zealand after a season on the ice.

One of these was vulcanologist Philip Kyle, just back from his eighth trip to Anarctica. Kyle had a series of cliff-hanging stories to tell his old friends at Victoria University—about a season of violent eruptions, gigantic lava bombs, scientific progress, and plans temporarily foiled. He was already organizing a field party for another expedition to Mount Erebus later in the year.

Kathy listened with growing interest. Suddenly, her thesis about a quiet little volcano in the North Island seemed very tame. As Kyle talked, a detailed picture of Mount Erebus grew in her imagination.

When Philip Kyle tells people about his favorite volcano he can draw an instant diagram of the summit and the unique double crater. He sketches in the side crater—an ancient bowl-shaped depression, now quiet and partially filled in. Then he focuses on the active cone, the almost perfectly circular main crater. Inside that, he points to a deep, cylindrical hole that is the inner crater.

"That's where all the activity is," he explains. "If you want to get to the hot lava and gases, you have to go into the inner crater."

Getting to the gases is essential to the work of many vulcanologists. For more than a century, scientists have tried to understand the original composition of volcanic gases. Some chemical analyses have been made, but the results are still debated by scientists and no overall picture has emerged.

A top researcher in this field is Haroun Tazieff, a French

Twin craters of Mount Erebus seen from the air

vulcanologist who has spent some thirty years collecting and studying gas samples from the world's active volcanoes. For a long time, he was puzzled by the absence of any consistent results. "The proportions of the various substances," he wrote, "seem to be entirely capricious."

Tazieff added that the biggest problem he faces is to trap the gases close to their original state, before they mingle with other gases in the air. In order to do this, a scientist has to be inside the crater, close to a vent or lava pool where the gases originate.

Of the thousands of active volcanoes on earth, only two or three have lakes of molten lava. Erebus is one of these, but nobody knew about it until the southern summer of 1972–73 when a New Zealand party, including Philip Kyle and Werner Giggenbach, made the discovery.

The two men were part of an expedition that had ambitious plans for descending into the inner crater. Up until that time, nobody had ever been inside the main crater, let alone the inner one. Giggenbach was determined to collect gases at their source and to study their chemical composition. Kyle, a geologist studying the composition of the lava, was fascinated by his companion's daring plan. It wasn't easy.

"We were green," he said later. "We didn't know what to expect. We went there with a winch and other heavy equipment, planning to go down into the inner crater. It didn't work. The volcano was erupting and we didn't have the equipment or knowledge to carry out the whole plan."

"It wasn't safe," Giggenbach explained. "Eruptions occur in a random manner. They may be five minutes apart or a half-hour apart. It's impossible to predict. Our chances of being hit were maybe one in five, but it wasn't safe to go into the inner crater during the eruptions. We had to give up that idea—temporarily."

"The expedition certainly wasn't a total loss," Kyle added. "We did accomplish two things that year."

Their first accomplishment was to climb down into the main crater. "That was an achievement in itself," Kyle said. "Werner and John Shorland, a field assistant from DSIR, became the first people ever to get inside the main crater. Once we had done that, we knew it was feasible to go into the inner crater—if the volcano would stay quiet long enough."

Their second achievement was the discovery of molten lava in the inner crater. As they stood on the crater rim looking down into the steam-filled inner pits, there was a brief clearing of steam. They noticed an intermittent red glow from the gray surface of what appeared to be two pools of highly viscous lava. As they watched, the gray material started to bulge in spots. Then the bulges broke, puffing and spattering, exposing the underlying bright-orange fire.

The lava pools, they noted, measured from twenty to thirty meters across. In subsequent years they were to see the lava spread and grow into a lake that filled more than half of the inner crater.

"We finally accepted the fact that we probably couldn't do it by ourselves," Kyle remembered. "We had to call on somebody who had a lot of experience getting into volcanoes. So I wrote to Tazieff and said we needed his expertise."

That letter had led to the first international expedition to Erebus in the 1974–75 season. Tazieff's French team joined a group of New Zealanders and Americans in a second attempt to conquer the inner crater. But the volcano protested, hurling lava bombs and steam at the invaders.

Giggenbach tried once more in 1975–76, but once again he was driven back by violent eruptions. Tazieff had returned to the summit in 1977–78, the season just ending when Kathy Cashman heard Philip Kyle's account of his adventures.

It had happened again, Kyle reported. The scientists had failed to get into the inner crater. Tazieff and Giggenbach were especially disappointed, but they hadn't given up. They would, Kyle said, return to Erebus in the summer of 1978–79. He expected to be there, too, but his plans were still preliminary. Since 1976 he had been working in the United States at the Ohio State University's Institute of Polar Studies. Now he was on his way back to Ohio to organize a new research project. He might, he said, need two more field assistants.

Kathy spoke up immediately, before she had time to lose her nerve. Kyle promised to let her know.

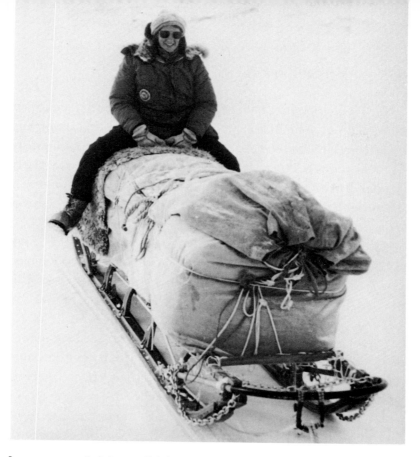

In a caravan of sledges pulled by snowmobiles, Kathy Cashman traveled 500 miles across the polar plateau.

"The answer came in July," Kathy recalled. "I guess it was a matter of being in the right place at the right time. I was hired as a field assistant for the Ohio party."

After that, things happened fast. Kathy tried to keep her mind on her master's thesis, but visions of snow-covered volcanoes refused to be ignored. In October she saw Mount Erebus for the first time—from a helicopter. It would be six more weeks before she actually stood on the summit. Until then she would be traveling in a caravan of sledges pulled by snowmobiles— five hundred miles across the polar plateau.

Navy helicopters dropped the small field party and their
equipment at their first campsite in the icy desert, about 150
miles from McMurdo. After that, they were on their own, except
for radio contact. The temperature, when they landed, was thirty
degrees below zero and the wind was so wild that it was a
real struggle for them to set up their little pyramid-shaped Scott
tents.

"Our party included just four people," Kathy said. "Philip
Kyle was the leader. Harry Keys, a New Zealand geochemist
who had worked with Kyle before, was our alpine expert. Bill
MacIntosh, a Colorado geologist, was our mechanic. I was the
only field assistant."

These modern explorers were heading into areas never before
disturbed by human visitors. They would climb remote *nuna-
taks*—exposed peaks of mountains long buried under layers of
ice nearly three miles thick. Rock samples from these peaks
could be analyzed later to reveal details about the history of
the continent.

Their days fell into a pattern. A radio call to McMurdo was
first on the schedule every morning. Then they melted snow
for water and thawed their food for breakfast, taking turns with
all the housekeeping chores.

"After breakfast," Kathy recalled, "two people would brave
the cold to start packing the sledges while the other two packed
up the gear inside the tents. Once the sledges were packed,
we set out and traveled all day—with brief stops for snacks or
warm-up—until we were too tired to go on. Then we reversed
the morning's procedure—unpacking sledges, setting up tents,
lighting stoves, and preparing dinner."

Travel by sledge was surprisingly bumpy, Kathy discovered.
The hard-packed snow had been shaped by the winds into ridges

and unexpected forms that reminded her of "armies of snow-sculptured gnomes." On sunny days the air was so clear and cold that it sometimes "sparkled with the diamond reflections of thousands of tiny ice crystals."

"If the weather wasn't too bad, we'd take the time to build an igloo with blocks of wind-packed snow," Kathy said. "The consistency was about like styrofoam, so we could easily saw it into building blocks. After a bit of experimenting we learned how to trim corners to fit. Pretty soon we could build an igloo with surprising ease."

As a geologist, Kathy found distinct advantages in Antarctic field work, in spite of the hostile climate. "There are no bugs, no rain, no trees or shrubs to get in the way," she said.

By mid-December, the sledges were heavily loaded with bags of rock samples and the adventurers returned to McMurdo. A few days later they were halfway to the summit of Mount Erebus, camping at Fang Glacier for the customary two days of acclimatization. Erebus is more than two miles high. People who make the ascent all at once—by aircraft, with no stops along the way—often suffer from altitude sickness. Kathy and her companions took no chances with symptoms that could range from nausea to unconsciousness.

When they arrived at the summit camp, on December 21, they found five New Zealanders and their French guest, Haroun Tazieff, already at work. Giggenbach was there. So was Colin Monteath, an experienced climber and safety expert who had, for several years, conducted survival courses for New Zealanders and Americans in Antarctica.

Monteath told the new arrivals about the events of the past three days. The party had made repeated attempts to get into the inner crater, but everything had gone wrong. The winds were unfavorable. Humidity was unusually high. The volcano had erupted—sometimes six times in one day—sending huge bombs into the main crater. One of the bombs littering the crater floor was a boulder nearly fifteen feet across. A smaller one had hit a coil of nylon rope and burned it through.

During the next two days, Kathy learned to handle the pulley ropes. Tazieff and Giggenbach were still waiting for the volcano and the weather to stay quiet long enough for a descent into the inner crater. Two days before Christmas, Tazieff's time ran out and he returned to Scott Base without completing his experiments. Giggenbach didn't give up.

That afternoon the wind died down. The volcano had been quiet for fourteen hours and Colin Monteath announced that he was going to try once more to make the descent. He would test the ropes and inspect the crater wall to see if they were safe. Wearing a helmet, in case of flying bombs, and carrying a gas mask, Monteath became the first person ever to go into the inner crater. It was an hour later that Giggenbach made his descent—and when he was about four-fifths of the way down, the volcano erupted.

The violent explosions that interrupted Giggenbach's experiments stopped as abruptly as they began. During the next few days there were more rumblings and eruptions, but the campers on the summit were busy with festive preparations.

It was a White Christmas—Mount Erebus style. The New Zealanders prepared a feast from the frozen provisions on hand, including a leg of lamb as the main course. Leg of lamb with a difference.

"They wrapped it in foil," Kathy explained, "then they put it into a cloth bag and hung it over one of the volcano's steam

Kathy Cashman and her traveling companion, Paddington Bear, arrived at Mount Erebus in time for Christmas in 1979.

vents to cook for twenty-four hours. It's a method they learned from the Maoris—the original New Zealanders—who were cooking their food over steam vents in the North Island long before they ever saw Captain Cook. When the Maoris have a feast they call it a *hangi*—so that's what we called our Christmas party."

That was Kathy Cashman's first Christmas away from home. A year later, Christmas, 1979, she was back on the summit of Erebus, laden with presents for her New Zealand friends, ready to wrap another leg of lamb for the annual *hangi.*

Sixteen

EQUAL PARTNERS

"Since the world began," said Jennie Darlington in *My Antarctic Honeymoon,* "women have seen that burning, distant look [in men's eyes], hinting of faraway places, and been afraid. For exploration is a male compulsion, generally beyond feminine comprehension."

Not beyond the comprehension of women like the new explorers now working for science in Antarctica. The frontiers they explore in university laboratories are linked to remote and rugged geographical frontiers. These women hike over glaciers, camp in windy deserts, dive under the ice, fly for hours over unexplored mountain ranges, and enter steaming volcano craters.

By the 1980s, women had become equal partners in Antarctic research and were accepted in other jobs previously reserved for men—even on construction crews. When the U.S. Navy announced, in 1979, that "qualified women volunteers" would be assigned to Antarctic duty in winter—as well as summer—the last barrier fell.

Navy women had already demonstrated their ability to cope

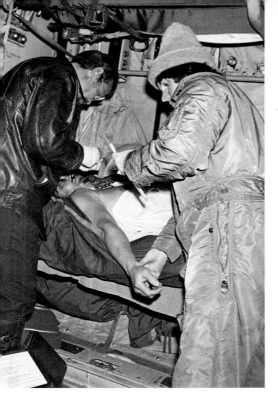

Aboard rescue plane, Lt. Commander Caroline Deegan, Navy flight surgeon, treats a man injured in Soviet air crash.

with emergencies in Antarctica. Lieutenant Commander Caroline Deegan, the Navy flight surgeon based at McMurdo in the austral summer of 1978–79, didn't just dispense aspirin and Band-Aids. In the middle of the busy season, she became part of a dramatic rescue operation.

A Soviet transport plane crashed when an engine failed on takeoff from Molodezhnaya, the largest Russian station in Antarctica. The pilot, copilot, and a passenger were killed and eleven others were injured. Five of the men were so seriously hurt that the commander of the Russian station called for help from the U.S. Navy to evacuate the men to a New Zealand hospital equipped to handle brain injuries. Dr. Caroline Deegan and two medical orderlies gathered up their equipment and flew to Molodezhnaya, on the other side of the Antarctic continent.

It was a long and difficult flight. The pilot, commanding officer

LEFT: Martha Wolfe, in wet suit, prepares to go under the ice. RIGHT: Martha Kane keeps track of changing flow patterns of cosmic rays.

of the Navy's VXE-6 Squadron in Antarctica, was handicapped by heavy fog, high winds, and the need to land at the South Pole for refueling. But they made it to Molodezhnaya in less than twelve hours.

Under Dr. Deegan's supervision, a makeshift hospital had been set up in the cargo area of the big Hercules aircraft. At Molodezhnaya, a Soviet doctor came aboard with the patients and worked with Dr. Deegan until they reached McMurdo. He accompanied the injured men on the last leg of the flight to New Zealand while Caroline Deegan, after a sleepless day and night, was surrounded by friends who wanted to hear about the rescue.

"She was very popular with everybody at McMurdo," said Audrey Haschemeyer, who was there at the same time. "She's really good. People feel she's genuinely interested in their health. The men didn't seem to mind at all that their doctor was a woman."

Dr. Haschemeyer and her colleague, Rita Mathews, said that they felt no negative discrimination at all during their seasons at McMurdo.

"The old attitude is outdated," Audrey said. "We received very warm treatment—were respected as scientists. If there are any male chauvinists still around, we didn't see them. Now that more women are working in Antarctica, I think it has become a more normal human society—just different from a single-sex society."

Even at the South Pole, where women had never spent a winter until Dr. Michele Raney became the year-round physician, women now fill a variety of jobs, summer and winter. When Dr. Raney flew home in November, 1979, another woman arrived to stay through 1980. Martha Kane, a graduate student from the University of Delaware, would spend a year monitoring interplanetary weather—keeping track of changing flow patterns of cosmic rays near the earth.

Other women also arrived at the Pole to work during the summer. Julie Ann Samson, a physics student from Albany, New York, did research at the clean air facility—measuring the concentration of aerosols in the air. A letter from this young explorer arrived in an envelope impressively stamped with the return address in bold, black capital letters:

AMUNDSEN
SCOTT
SOUTH-POLE
STATION
ANTARCTICA
90°SO BOTTOM OF THE WORLD

The letter is as cheerful and chatty as a report from a daughter in college. "It took six days and thirty-five hours on various planes, but I'm here!" she began. "The people here at Pole are great! I've enjoyed every minute of my stay thus far."

Inside the Clean Air Facility at South Pole Station, Julie Ann Samson measures aerosol content of air samples.

Her fellow residents, she reported, ranged in age from twenty-two to sixty-five years. There were only forty-five people there and four of them were women.

"One is on the construction crew," Julie wrote. "There is also a woman GFA [general field assistant] . . . from Idaho. Martha Kane, the only female [to] winter over, works on cosmic rays and I work at the clean air facility on atmospheric physics."

Life at the Pole is not all work, Julie discovered. In her spare time she found plenty to do—from golf and sledding to movies and dancing.

"Recently we held the First Annual South Pole Golf Tournament. It was only one hole, 237 yards long, and they even raked and colored the snow green to make a putting green. Prizes were awarded that night . . . I tied for next-to-last place and won half a six-pack of some terrible beer."

A "sock hop" in the gym sounded like a weekend event on some college campus. The men were invited, Julie said, but the women—all four of them—were required to attend. Then there was the fifth annual Pole Bowl football game on New Year's Day—science team *vs* support crew. From time to time there were volleyball, basketball, and softball games. Some of the activities were more daring.

"Dome-sliding is great fun, but probably quite dangerous, too," Julie wrote. "Most of the buildings here are covered by a huge geodesic dome . . . often used for dome sliding. One climbs to the top of the dome and either 1, 2, 3, or 4 people hop on a banana sled and away you go!"

Quieter entertainment included movies shown in the "90° South Club"—"usually very recent movies." Julie's enthusiasm seemed to extend to everything about her South Pole experience—the people, the scenery, the work, and the fun. She was especially impressed by the democracy of the small community.

"The nicest aspect of life at the South Pole is the fact that everyone is equal. I didn't feel this was the case at McMurdo, but Pole is different. . . . From the most famous principal investigator to the lowest-paid GFA—and between men and women—we're all equal. We all wear the same clothes, eat the same food and are here for basically the same reason. Without the support crew, the scientists could not survive and without the scientists there would be no need for the support crew. Everyone respects everyone else. . . ."

When there was enough snow, adventurous sledders used the shiny dome of the South Pole Station for sliding.

"Equal partners" on the University of Minnesota team capture a seal near McMurdo.

As equal partners, women who work in Antarctica today may be puzzled by Jennie Darlington's conclusion, more than thirty years ago: "Taking everything into consideration, I do not think women belong in Antarctica." But be fair to Jennie. It was a rough life she shared on Stonington Island in 1947. There were no showers, no movies, no frozen lobster, no organized sports. And she was there as a wife—not as an independent researcher with important work to do.

When Sister Mary Odile Cahoon flew to McMurdo in 1974, as one of the first two women ever to spend a winter there, she foresaw the new role of women in Antarctica.

"If women are in science—and science is there," she said, "then women need to go there as scientists."

INDEX